SERENITY
1 84576 082 4

Published by
Titan Books
A division of
Titan Publishing Group Ltd
144 Southwark St
London
SE1 0UP

First edition September 2005
1 3 5 7 9 10 8 6 4 2

Conceptual Artists: Matt Codd, Tim Flattery, Robert M. Kalafut, Josh Middleton,
Wil Madoc Rees and Leinil Yu.
© 2005 Universal Studios Licensing LLLP. *Serenity* © Universal Studios. All Rights Reserved.

Acknowledgements
The publishers would like to thank everyone who helped make this book possible, including Abbie
Bernstein; Michael Boretz; Dawn Ahrens, Veronika Beltran, Cindy Chang, Julie Chebbi, Afsoon Razavi,
Jennifer Sandberg and Angie Sharma at Universal; the cast and crew of *Serenity*; and of course Joss
Whedon, without whom there'd be no signal in the first place.

Did you enjoy this book? We love to hear from our readers. Please e-mail us at:
readerfeedback@titanemail.com or write to Reader Feedback at the above address. To subscribe
to our regular newsletter for up-to-the-minute news, great offers and competitions,
email: **titan-news@titanemail.com**

Visit our website: www.titanbooks.com

A CIP catalogue record for this title is available from the British Library.

Printed and bound in the USA.

THE OFFICIAL VISUAL COMPANION

With an Introduction and the
Motion Picture Screenplay
by Joss Whedon

TITAN BOOKS

CONTENTS

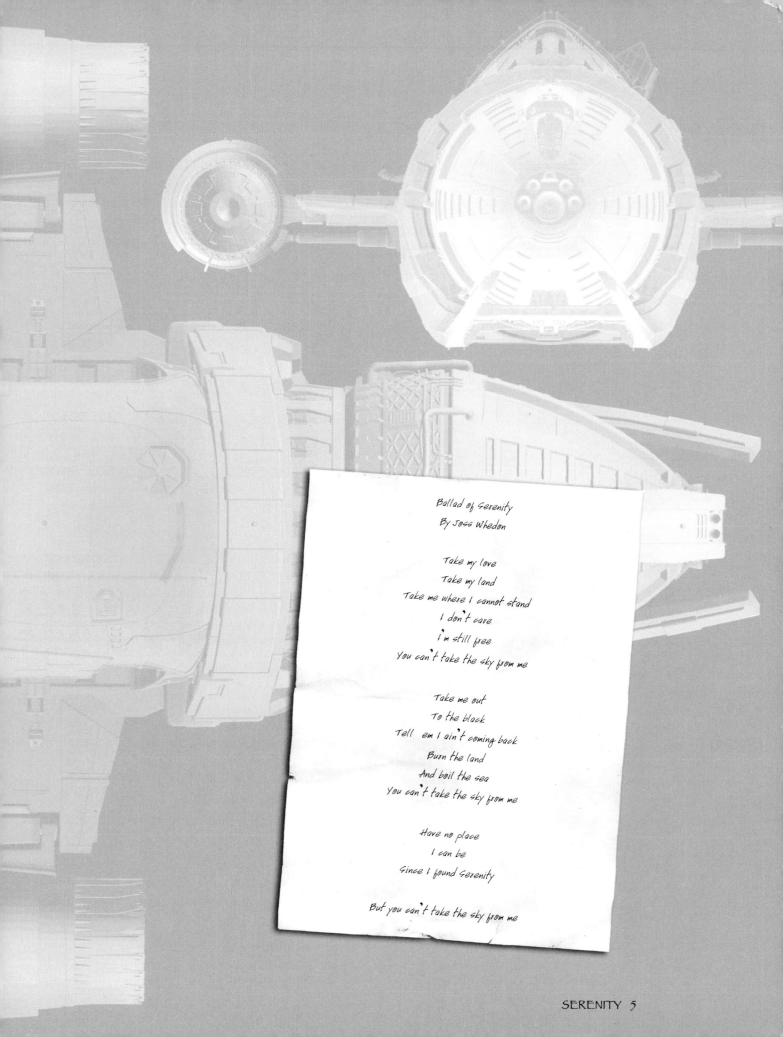

Ballad of Serenity
By Joss Whedon

Take my love
Take my land
Take me where I cannot stand
I don't care
I'm still free
You can't take the sky from me

Take me out
To the black
Tell em I ain't coming back
Burn the land
And boil the sea
You can't take the sky from me

Have no place
I can be
Since I found Serenity

But you can't take the sky from me

INTRODUCTION

BY JOSS WHEDON

It's in here.

The truth. The reality — of making a film, of imagining a universe, of creation. Collaboration. The changes. The fights. The drunken brawls, the on-set back-stabbing, the desperate romances, firey crashes and the endless, relentless boobies.

Okay. So, sorry about that last paragraph. That was just to get people to buy the book. You know, they're glancing it over in the store... you throw in a few key-words that spark a buyer's interest. In all honesty, there wasn't actually any collaboration.

But there is something exciting in this book, and it is in fact truth. A glimpse of the truth of how much ded-icated effort and random strangeness goes into this kind of endeavor. An unfiltered look into the mind of a filmmaker. Sadly, that filmmaker is me. But if you're holding the book, you might hold the film, or some character from it, dear, and this book will broaden your understanding of every aspect of the subject. You might share with me the overwhelming, obses-sive love of this world, of these characters, of the actors who played them and the crew who put them on the screen. A love so fierce it usurped my life — which was going along fine, thank you very much — for years to put this film together. Tortured months writing, delightful months filming, more tortured months editing. I have been humbled by the experi-ence of making this, but luckily most of the humbling happened during editing and there's no chapter on that! So you totally won't ever know! Sweet!

I love this movie. You get that already. Do I love this book? I do. It has the script, a miracle of ungainly cre-ation, like a Fabergé egg made with a blacksmith's hammer. It has the Mee-mo's, which I wrote in a frenzy of late night inspiration and which helped me understand the work I was about to undertake even as they confused and frightened everyone around me. (So we're clear here: it's pronounced 'Mee-Moes'. A 'memo' is too small a thing to contain that much pre-tension.) And of course there's photos, all of which I love that do not contain in any way me. (Only my wife can make me look good. Some of you know how that works.) Add the extraordinary patience of Abbie Bernstein in our long, rambling-is-too-kind-a-word conversations and you really do have a scriptbook that is a good deal more than just that. You want another piece of *Serenity*? Of the goofy, transcendent joy that was its creation?

It's in here.

Joss. 5/31/05

TAKING BACK THE SKY

Opposite: The crew of Serenity as the story opens (left to right): Jayne (Adam Baldwin), Kaylee (Jewel Staite), Wash (Alan Tudyk), Zoe (Gina Torres), Mal (Nathan Fillion), Simon (Sean Maher), and River (Summer Glau). The movie also of course features ex-crewmembers Inara (Morena Baccarin) and Shepherd Book (Ron Glass).

Below: Writer/director Joss Whedon.

How similar is the *Serenity* screenplay to the movie?

JOSS WHEDON: The script reflects the movie, absolutely.

How did the idea for *Firefly* evolve?

After season three of *Buffy* [summer of 1999]. I went to England for my two-week vacation with my wife [Kai Cole]. We'd wake up, go see a play in the evening, then read all night, then go to sleep all day. I ended up seeing eight plays and reading ten books in the space of about twelve days. So it was very heady. Westerns are one of my favorite genres, but not one that I had any ambition of making. Probably because they're usually very quiet, and that's something I've never been very good at being — they have breathing room, they have small moments and they take their time. But science fiction is absolutely an obsession, and what happened when I read [Michael Shaara's Civil War book] *The Killer Angels* was not so much thinking about Western genre as about the experience of immigrants and pioneers moving west, the dangers and the desperation of the

kind of person who'd go with their family and babies into unknown territory, where nobody wanted them, with nothing but what they could carry either on their backs or in their wagons. I thought putting it in a setting of a science fiction show would service everything that I wanted. One, the glory and the glamour and the excitement of seeing other worlds and quite frankly spaceships, and two, really getting into the lives of everyday people when [the phrase 'everyday people'] meant something very different, when it meant the kind of strength and resilience and toughness and sometimes moral ambiguity that none of us is faced with nowadays. I guess the classic 'me' portion of that is simply that I so desperately needed a vacation, I was so completely burnt out, on my first night, in a foreign land, I wrote the entire outline for the pilot. Which I guess is my idea of a vacation [laughs].

The basic tenet was that it was [analogous to the post-United States Civil War] Reconstruction era. Mal had fought for the South — not for slavery, I can't stress that enough [laughs], but for [the losing side]. The next book that I read after *The Killer Angels* was about Jewish partisan fighters who had fought in the Warsaw uprising [during WWII] and some of the things they tried to pull off after the war. And that's when I realized there was no piece of history that was not useful [to] the story I was going to tell. I even had my brother Sam, who worked for years as a first mate on a boat salmon fishing in Alaska, come and tell stories to my [*Firefly*] writers about ships suddenly sinking with all hands, finding dead people in the water, just because that's the closest thing we have to life on the edge in this country right now. I read a lot of letters — there are a couple of collections of letters [from] around 1849 of women pioneers crossing into the West that are absolutely fascinating in their complete deadpan acceptance of the abhorrent conditions.

How did you devise the singular dialogue style?

The patois with which [the characters] speak is very made-up. It has a lot of Western in it. I took a lot of Shakespeare, some Pennsylvania Dutch from the turn of the century, some Irish, any colloquialism that fit in their mouths, plus a lot of Chinese, which they all cursed me for — in English, because the Chinese is too damn hard to remember. People talk about it as Western, but actually, with a healthy dollop of made-up Joss talk, it's basically based on everything. A very influential book for me was *Tillie: A Mennonite Maid*, a story of the Pennsylvania Dutch from the turn of the

century which has wonderful phrasings in it, and then
of course, Elizabethan English always works its way
into my work, because I'm a little obsessed with it. I'm
also terribly fond of Victorian literature and of
Dickens. It could be something out of hip-hop. If it
rings true, it goes in. And if it doesn't, hoo-boy, you
can tell.

**How did you decide on China as the other superpower
in the story's universe?**

Well, have you seen China lately? China is as big and
powerful as any nation on this Earth, and will be more
powerful than the United States real soon. And my wife
lived in China for a while and so I had learned a little bit
about it from her, and mostly what I had learned was
what an important power it was. My feeling was, I would
create a kind of utopia in which America and China,
being the two great powers, came up together and com-
bined their technologies to get everybody off the
depleted Earth and colonize the Central Planets and
formed the Alliance. And I also loved the fact that,
again, Westerns — and this is something that was very
much stressed in the '70s, but you can also see them in
John Ford movies, were immigrant stories. The Wild
West was full of people from the Far East, and so the
mixture of those two cultures — that's what history is,

it's culture in a blender, and so to take those two and
juxtapose them, the idea that every nobody speaks
fluent Chinese to me is kind of delightful and not
actually unrealistic.

Was *Firefly* initially conceived as a TV series?

This was designed to be a TV series, because I wanted to
tell the boring stories about Han Solo smuggling when
he wasn't involved with the Rebellion, I wanted to tell
the stories about people who live in between and the
stories themselves that live in between greater stories.
After the initial idea for the pilot, I increased the cast
from five to nine members so that I could generate stories from within the ship and not have to constantly go
out to new and exciting worlds and guest stars that we
couldn't afford, and I made every planet Planet Earth so
that we didn't have to go to Yucca Flats and pretend it
was an alien planet every other week. It was a deliberately television idea.

I wanted to tell mundane stories, but at the same
time — and this was also part of the network's hope — I
wanted an overarching, ongoing building story that
would eventually culminate in a bit of an epic tale that
our people could become involved in, centrally or
peripherally, but that we would see the grand scheme of
what was going on and secrets would be revealed and

people would be chased. I wanted the show to live in the spaces in between actions, spaces that people don't really deal with, that TV gives you the opportunity to do. But not Fox TV. They wanted more of an action show, with more momentum, and so since that was also a part of these people's lives, I didn't feel like it was a betrayal of the vision of the show to amp it up a little.

What were the original concepts for the main characters?

When I actually realized I was going to make this thing, it had already been living in my head for awhile. I dragged out my tiny little notebook that I scribbled on. I then sat down and said, 'Okay, I really need the ensemble on board this ship, because I can't afford to leave it,' so I just started drawing them out. And the process of creating characters is creating differences. It's finding 'What purpose does each character serve that's different than every other character?' So you never repeat yourself."

I would say the only absolute definite [character in the initial premise] was Mal [Nathan Fillion]. Zoe was a man, and then there was a Kaylee character. Mal was supposed to be the hero, but in the loosest sense of the word, everything that a hero is not, and everything by the way that *my* hero is not, because he's somewhat of a reactionary, he's a conservative kind of Libertarian guy. I've often said that if Mal and I sat down to dinner, we'd have a terrible time. I don't actually agree with most of what he says, but he's the person who has to be unutterably tough and sometimes cruel in order to survive, and that to me is a fascinating character, whether or not we'd get along.

When you have people that far out and you're dealing with culture as much as any science fiction does, faith became very important, the idea of religion and belief systems. That's why I wanted Shepherd Book [Ron Glass]. Shepherd Book is somebody I would probably get along famously with, except we don't agree about anything. It's the classic thing to have a preacher on board your stagecoach — I don't mean *Stagecoach*, I mean original idea of my own [laughs] — but I wanted to have a voice for the other side. Shepherd Book interested me as a character, too. Like Giles [on *Buffy*], he was never supposed to be just the man who told you what was going on.

Inara's [Morena Baccarin] character originally was a whore, something very *Deadwood*. My wife said, 'Why not do something more in the style of a geisha and make her the most educated person on the ship, instead of just an oppressed, pathetic creature?' And then, of course, people [said], 'What a typical boy fantasy.' And I thought, 'Yeah, that's my wife!' Inara obviously [is] the opposite of Mal, she represents the Alliance and everything that's good about it — enlightenment, education, self-possession, feminism. She was a foil for Mal that inevitably would become romantic.

Jayne [Adam Baldwin] — bad guy. I never meant for him to be so lovable so quickly. You found yourself going, 'Oh!' This is the Cordelia of the bunch, the guy who's going to say what everybody's thinking.' I wanted somebody on the ship that we absolutely could not trust, but who in a pinch was good in a fight, but that as a person, we always were waiting for him to stab us in the back.

If you gave [Baldwin] something, he always wanted to know where it came from and where it was going and how he could use it to relate to the people around him. [Baldwin] will give you an analysis of what he thinks the scene is, every little thing. There's so much stuff [Baldwin discovered] that was very useful. He always followed through. And he gets very sexual about his gun — but only when he's being Jayne, not Adam.

Zoe [Gina Torres] was there to represent a side of Mal that nobody else really understood — his honor and the fact that he was such a good leader that this person who is happily married and completely at peace with herself would still follow him into these serious and sometimes dumb situations, because he had been that important to her in the war, and that just gave Mal cred.

The idea of Wash [Alan Tudyk] — well, obviously, a humorous, self-deprecating guy is always going to make his way into my shows. [Wash is] an absolute contrast to Zoe, yet a perfect mate for her. Rather than playing out every little romance in its infancy the way shows usually do, I thought it would be nice to show a happily married couple, who would have their fights and their troubles but would stay married. That was actually one of the sticking points when I sold the show. The last thing that Fox said was, 'We will pick up the show, but they can't be married.' And I said, 'Then don't pick up the show, because in my show, these people are married. And it's important to the show.' So I asked them not to pick up the show. But then they did anyway. But then they buried it. But that's another story.

Below: Serenity's happily married couple, Zoe and Wash.

A BRIEF HISTORY OF THE UNIVERSE
circa 2507 A. D.

By Joss Whedon

Earth-That-Was couldn't handle the growing population and resource needs of humankind. Amazingly enough, instead of wiping itself out, the human race rose to the challenge of finding a new home for the species. A nearby star was located, home to dozens of planets and hundreds of moons, almost all of which had enough mass and solidity to be templates for new earths. Through giant atmosphere processing plants, terraforming technologies, gravity regulation and the introduction of every known form of Earthlife, each planet became its own little (or in some cases, huge) Earth. Every person willing and able to leave the Earth migrated to the new system. An entire generation never even saw the outside of a spaceship, the journey took so long. But the planets were ready for habitation (despite the odd quirk of nature or miscalculation on a few) and civilization as we knew it began to rebuild. The work started on the two largest, most central planets, SIHNON and LONDINIUM.

On Earth-That-Was, the two ruling powers were once known as America and China. Though their empires remained separate, the two powers worked together throughout the colonization process, their cultures — as so many had — melding at many levels. Londinium, called so after the Roman name for England's capital (a country long before annexed by America in a somewhat ironic reversal), represented what was once the American Empire. Sihnon ("SEE-non", a bastardization of Sino, our word for 'Chinese') was the new China, basically. These two powers, still working in harmony, grew at once into the most populous and advanced civilizations in the new galaxy.

'Advanced' meant just that: these were enlightened cultures, with respect for all non-aggressive religious beliefs (though the main religion on both planets was Buddhism). Literacy levels were at 94%. Average lifespan was 120. Public Service was not law — it was simply an ingrained part of the people's ethos. And pot was totally legal (though I probably won't stress that). (In fact, forget I said it.) The point is, certain social mores had evolved (whether forwards or backwards is a matter of opinion) beyond our modern conceptions. As, for example, sex. Prostitution as we understand it had long since been abolished by the legalization and strict federal regulation of the sex trade. "Companion" houses were set up throughout the central planets. No house could ever be run by a man. No Companion could ever be coerced into

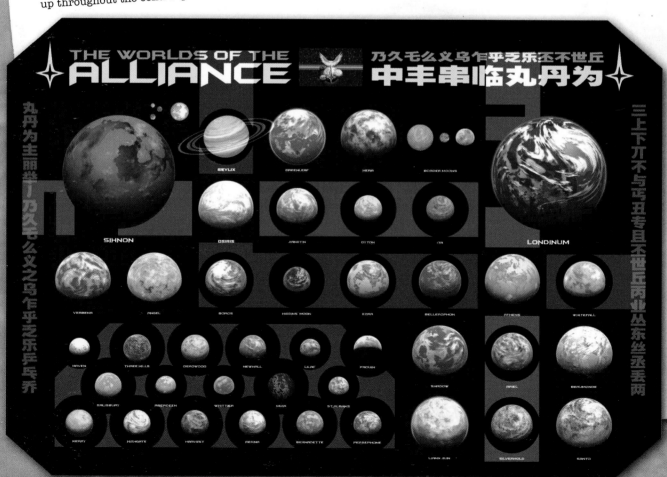

accepting a client. Companions trained in all the arts, extremely well schooled. They lived not unlike Nuns, worked not unlike Geishas, and often rose to political or social prominence when they retired.

Such was life on the central planets: among them Sihnon, Londinium, and Osiris, (where Simon and River Tam grew up). On the outer planets, things were a mite different.

The thing is, we had enough worlds to go around, but not enough resources. And people didn't exactly stop making babies. The outer planets, the worlds and moons that hadn't been chosen to house the new civilization — they were the destination for the poorer, more extreme, the pioneers. They traveled out to the nearest planet someone hadn't claimed yet and started turning their rockets into roofs. Building off whatever the land had been shaped to provide them with. Some of these people were brought near to savagery by the conditions they encountered. Some were hard-working, independent folk who didn't want their lives mapped out for them before they'd lived them. Didn't want convenience. Some were orthodox in their beliefs to the point where they were not comfortable among non-believers, and wanted whole worlds where they would not be slowly homogenized into society. And some had reason to avoid the law.

There were troubles. There were famines, there were wars — the human race didn't get better or smarter just 'cause they had made scientific leaps. Things were definitely more peaceful among the Central Planets, but that peace was bought at a price. Nothing resembling totalitarianism, but a certain regulation of existence that would not sit well with some. And even among these planets, conflicts over resources, trade, and political influence strained the civil relations of sister nations. In an effort to unite and quell this conflict, the Central Planets formed the ALLIANCE, a governing structure that unified them all under one governing body, the PARLIAMENT. The few members represent-ed each planet, and worked in genuine harmony to fulfil each planet's various needs, economically and politically. In harmony, and very often, in secrecy.

For we are nothing more than humans, however high we reach. The Parliament ruled over people with fairness and intelligence, but also with a strong army and a wary eye toward any insurrection. The MILITARY COUNCIL worked under the Parliament to deliver swift, effective control of any real unrest among them or their neighbors. And even beyond the knowledge of the Military council were other bodies, secret bodies... human experimentation. Spies. Assassins. Schemes, secret up to the highest level, to get people to behave. To improve.

The real trouble started when the Alliance started to look beyond its borders to the worlds around them. Partially out of a desire to see life improved there (and it WAS often unnecessarily barbaric), to bring all the planets into the fold of enlightenment, and partially out of a simple imperialistic wish for control and need for resources off-limits to them, the Parliament — and the Allied planets as a whole — decided that EVERY planet should become part of their program. Should be an Alliance planet, whether they wanted to or not.

The War for Unification was the most devastating in human history. Outer planets such as Hera (where the battle of Serenity was fought), Persephone, and Shadow mustered forces — more than half volunteers — to stop what they felt to be nothing more than imperialist hegemony. For almost five years the war tore into the planets between the central ones and the rim worlds (fighting never reached such pissant moons as Whitefall or Beaumonde, nor did it touch Sihnon and Londinium, except in the odd protest or terrorist act). The forces of the Alliance had the technology and the weapons to overcome almost any foe. But they never expected the kind of resistance the other planets could provide. They did not expect so many men and women to still consider freedom worth dying for.

Malcolm Reynolds was on Shadow, living on a cattle ranch his mother ran, when he joined up. He was a smart kid but green. He joined out of belief and nothing more. Five years gone found his homeworld destroyed, his army beaten down and every shred of belief ripped out of him. He had made Sergeant by then, of the 57th Overlanders. Would have gone higher if he had ever kept a single opinion to himself. But he wasn't in the war to get a title. He was there to fight, and in the Battle of Serenity, waged for seven gruelling weeks on Hera, he fought like nobody else. Some say the valley was the bridge between the worlds, and that when it fell the Independents fell with it. Surely Mal believed it, for he and his held the valley for a good two weeks AFTER the Independent High Command had already surrendered.

When it was all done, there was some talk of holding the "Browncoats" such as Mal who had held Serenity Valley as war criminals, since the war had officially ended. They were held in camps for a short time, but the Alliance considered it an important gesture to free them. The strain of criminality never left those few thousand — but in some quieter circles, the legend of their tenacity made them heroes.

Among those few thousand was Corporal Zoe Alleyne, also of the 57th Overlanders. She had been career Army, the opposite of Mal, but she had fought under him for the last two and a half years of the war, in more than a dozen campaigns. She also had the distinction of being the only other member of the 57th to survive Serenity. When Mal decided to get himself a little transport ship and head out to the rim worlds, to work the planets the Alliance would not truly be able to control, to settle down never and draw breath free... it never occurred to her not to follow him. It also never occurred to her that they would hire a pilot as annoying as Hoban Washburn, or that she would fall so completely in love with him. They were married not a year after they met, an occurrence that Mal considered ill-advised and slightly weird.

Wash turned out to be an extraordinary pilot, and they happened (it's a funny story) on a little prodigy of a mechanic, Kaywinnet Lee Frye, known as Kaylee. As sweet and cheerful as she was mechanical, she found the opportunity to be chief engineer (a title she used only to herself) on a firefly class ship to be beyond her best imaginings. Most folk wouldn't look twice at a firefly — it had since been replaced by sleeker, more efficient models, but she knew, as Mal did, that a firefly could hold up where others would buckle... that she could get in and out of places other ships couldn't, and quickly too... that she was just right for the kind of jobs nobody was supposed to be doing any more.

'Cause a lot of the work to be found on border planets was crime, and that was no problem for Mal. He expected it, and he prepared for it. He found himself a great lug of a mercenary in Jayne Cobb: mean, untrustworthy, and indispensable. On the flip side, they actually landed a passenger who could lend them respectability: A first rate companion, Inara Serra, who had left House Madrassa on Sihnon to work independently. She never did say why.

Then one day they took on a Shepherd named Book and a young Doctor from Osiris named Simon Tam, who had his sister River hidden in a cryogenic box for some damn reason. And that is, of course, another story.

Above: Framing a shot of Mal and Inara (Morena Baccarin) during the location filming for the Miranda sequence.

Kaylee [Jewel Staite], obviously, is the soul of the ship. Again, she's somebody who gives the captain cred because she likes him even when he's mean. And she sees the good in him, and in everything. [Kaylee] is kind of like [*Buffy*'s] Willow in the sense that [she's] the thing that connects everybody. And nobody doesn't like Kaylee. Anybody who doesn't — clearly out of their minds.

Simon [Sean Maher], like Inara, represents the sort of anti-Mal. [Simon is] an Alliance figure who had obviously been disillusioned by the Black Ops work that was going on and that was done to his sister, but somebody who would come up against Mal ideologically and practically a lot of the time.

River [Summer Glau] was the wild card [who] became the adolescent with superpowers, because apparently I can't ever write anything without an adolescent girl with superpowers, and I just have to accept that about myself and be at peace. In a weird way, she was coming to represent the audience voice, because she soaked in everything that everybody did so tactilely and so emotionally that she was almost kind of the narrator. But she was also the propulsion of what was going to happen, because she had a mystery behind her and the movie is about the mystery.

The original idea was, she's a cool psychic weapon and [the Alliance] want her back, and then when I started to map out the next few years of the series in all my naïve hilarity, I came upon what ultimately would be the plot of the movie, which [had the series continued] was supposed to take two years to develop and now takes a little under two hours. But that was always the idea. There was a secret that she was privy to that was going to affect the lives of our crew and in an enormous way, and that is exactly what happens.

Were there aspects of the characters that evolved because of how the actors played them?

I definitely ended up wanting to see a sweeter side of Jayne, because of how sweet and textured Adam was at being the roughneck, [and] a goofier side of Mal, because Nathan is a genius of comedy — he turned from Harrison Ford to Franklin Pangborn on a very

thin dime. And Nathan sometimes would be more poetically articulate about who Mal was than I would. I'd be like [whispers], 'Nathan, don't be so cool-sounding! Pretend *I* said that, okay?'

Everybody inhabited their characters so specifically the way I hoped they would that there [weren't problems with], 'Oh, I can't go here with this person.' I like to put my actors through the wringer. I like to ask everything of all of them. And then you find out who's really strong at one thing and who's really good for another, but basically, they came in and just inhabited those characters that I'd written to the point where I understood them better.

I never saw anybody jell like a family the way these people did, and that lasted not only throughout the TV show and throughout the movie, but in between, when there was little hope of being a movie. They stuck together and they stuck by me and they're dear friends and had a chemistry that was like a chemistry set.

Did you learn anything on *Firefly* that you hadn't learned about television or writing overall?

That sometimes it's better when you're under constant threat of cancellation, because it really brings out your best work. I had an experience that I'd never had before, and I've only ever had this happen once, but I literally had a scene write itself. I wrote stuff down and then looked at it and went, 'Where did that come from? What just happened?' So naturally, the character said, 'Where did that come from? What just happened?' Because Mal didn't understand why he was talking so much and neither did I. That was the scene where Mal is [talking with] Saffron, his new wife, in 'Our Mrs. Reynolds'. He started right into talking about his mother being a rancher and how she said, 'Brand the buyer, not the cattle — the buyer's the one likely to stray.' I've never met a cattleman, and I don't know if anybody's ever said that, but it sounded like it made sense to me. And I have no idea why he said it or why I wrote it, except that once I looked at it, I said, 'Well, that's a whole lot of talking for Mal.' And then I realized that Saffron was the kind of person — and there is this kind of person — who opens you up, makes you talk about yourself, finds your weaknesses and tries to set you against everybody else. So the thing really did just sort of get away from me. And then I understood why. That kind of ease, that kind of joy in every character, where it doesn't have to be a constructed joke, so it's not extremely difficult, but it does have a kind of rhythm to it that's almost poetical, it's just a joy to write. And that was different. That's part of why I loved the show so much and why I couldn't let go of it when it was cancelled.

When did you know *Firefly* the series was going away and when did you decide to write *Serenity*?

I knew *Firefly* was going away when [the Fox television executives] called me and told me it was. We were in the middle of shooting our last episode before Christmas [of

2002]. So I went on the stage, I gathered the cast and crew, I told them that we had been cancelled and that I would not rest until I found a new home for Serenity. And then I got all the people in my life at that point — my agent, my lawyer, Chris Buchanan, the head of my company, and Tim Minear, who was running *Firefly* with me — and said, 'I am not finished with this story. What can we do?' And there was a lot of head-scratching. It didn't look like it was going to have a TV reincarnation, so I was looking for somebody — the sets were still up. I literally had kept them up and had offered to pay for storing them myself, while I scrambled to find something. I called Barry Mendel, who I have known from before, who had a deal at Universal [and] flat-out asked him, 'Barry, what would you do in my shoes? I want to make a movie — it could be a TV movie, it could be a low-budget movie, it could be *anything*.' Barry mentioned it to [Universal executive] Mary [Parent], Mary saw the [*Firefly* episodes] and just signed on. Before I even had a story to tell, Mary said, 'I believe in this' and gave me all her support. So Universal came in where I thought nobody else would, and quite frankly, I'm not sure if anybody else would've, with absolute faith and has maintained it. It's been the easiest process in terms of dealing with a studio that I've ever had. And they turned it into — not a blockbuster, which is not what I was trying to make, but not a low-budget movie either. They wanted to make a real movie out of it. They wanted to give us the scope that the show could never have had. So all I had to do was come up with a story that was worth that.

Did the sales success of the *Firefly* DVDs help convince Universal to make *Serenity*?

They were definitely going ahead. It did not hurt at all. It definitely helped light a fire and make them go, 'Okay, we've really got something here.' It definitely helped them just be comfortable with the decisions they were making, but they really had been supporting us for quite some time already.

Did Universal give you a timetable for writing the script and/or going into production?

They had ideas about when they'd like to start shooting and I really only missed it by about eight months. I started writing and then they were like, 'Well, clearly we can start shooting in October.' So when we began shooting in June, I felt a little sheepish, but that was mostly due to the problems with my finishing the script.

Did any of the actors have a particularly vivid reaction on being told that *Serenity* was green-lighted?

Honestly, I can't remember. It's all like a blur. I think that Summer probably cried, but she does that every now and then. And Nathan wept like a little girl, of course. But it went straight in from 'We're making the movie' to 'And now we have to make deals with everybody.' [laughs] So the process just kept being the process. And everybody reacted much as you'd expect them to. Adam squealed like a little girl, as he so often does.

[Using the series cast] was never an issue. That was what the package was. [The Universal executives] really reviewed it — they watched the show, they watched every episode. And they said, 'We believe that this cast belongs up on a big screen.' Which is what I believe.

Was it difficult to adapt the *Firefly* premise into a movie?

I've never had an easier time writing than I did on *Firefly*. The hilarious irony being that I've never had a *harder* time writing than I did on *Serenity* because, having been given the opportunity to make this movie, I then had to make this movie worth making. And making a glorified episode of a TV show might rake in the dollars if the TV show is a huge hit, but it's not as satisfying to me as an artist, nor as satisfying to a studio. A movie is a very different animal than TV. Most people who say that are usually denigrating one of the mediums, and I think that neither of them is better than the other. They are as different as painting and pottery. It required readjustment narratively, because you have to tell the bullet points of the story and you're not going to be able to go off on bizarre tangents. I found myself in the very unenviable position of having to reintroduce all of the characters, to be true to everything that had happened before without repeating it or contradicting it, and making it palatable to an audience who has never seen the show. Now this becomes just incredibly difficult when you consider that not only are we dealing with nine characters who have already interacted, we're also dealing with an incredibly complex governmental and historical structure. There is the Alliance, the rule of the Alliance, the Parliament, the rebels, the Browncoats, the Independents, a lot of the Central Planets, the Outer Planets. In a way, it should be simple, but I didn't want it to be black and white; I didn't want it to be 'Empire evil, rebels good.' The whole point of this show and the movie is to say that things are not simple, that there is a moral gray area that we all live in that's very clear when we live on the frontier. And structurally, in terms of the screenplay — I've likened it to doing *Snow White and the Seven Dwarves*, only Snow White is told to go into the forest and we cut to a year later — she's been living with dwarves. That's a very hard structure to make work and make it feel like you're not dancing around something else, to make it feel like it's the right way to tell that story. Every phrase was painful, because every phrase had so much import. It wasn't like the TV show, where you could just throw something away [in the dialogue]. Every line had to be useful but not feel like a lesson. To hide that much information in a compelling story — let's just say I'm not anxious to do it again any time soon.

JOSS ON FRAME/LENS/PERSPECTIVE

This movie wasn't made. It was found. That's how I want it to feel: not grand, full of pomp and cinema, but immediate and real. Movies in general should feel like the people in them do, the way "Taxi Driver" puts you so firmly in Travis bickle's mind. (He crazy.) This movie is about an unhewn bunch; they don't stand on ceremony. Their frame is casual, unsteady, and just a little bit off. Because the story's being told by the girl in their midst, the girl with the mind that's not right.

It should feel so loose, so unschooled, that it almost completely hides the fact that it's a bit of a fairy tale.

I like wide lenses. My darling on TV was a 17mm, but with the giant super 35 I expect to back off to a 21 or so. I like to be in close, with the people, IN them. And they in their surroundings — ceilings, foreground pieces, enough depth to see everything. The longer lens, the shallow focus, the rack... they have a specific purpose. They're not common language. We'll tend to find them with River, to heighten her removal from those around her — sometimes to make the focus on her impossibly shallow, to watch her rock in and out of reality. (We might want to smoke a room occasionally just for her angles — to highlight said removal.)

I seldom frame things in the middle — and often like to cut faces in half in close-up. Depth will help us with such a large ensemble — I don't want to be racking to someone every time they speak, especially since these guys will be speaking over each other a lot. The "found" feeling of the film will also mean a lot of hand-held (or loose-wheeled/sandbagged dolly) that finds characters as they speak, not always landing perfectly before. Again, this much motion on the big screen probably means backing off from a 17, but we're definitely gonna be in the conversations with the same immediacy with which we'll be in, say, the mule. There will even be the occasional zoom, a piece of film vernacular I detest except in this instance. Here it feeds the random, docu-style casual frame I'm looking for, and it makes the frame as unMatrixy as possible. Zooming, searching, finding focus — all will be used (with discretion) and will also be seen in the CGI work. (And lens flares. I likes me some lens flares.) It's a holdover from the series' attempt to be present and unpretentious (and NOT Star Trek, which has been sanitized for your protection), but it's also specific to the film because of River. Because the story comes from her, and she is fragmented.

Cranes I use sparingly — they can really ANNOUNCE a shot and take you out of the moment. I love moving the camera, and there's a restlessness here that certainly justifies it. A master that works for a long while — in different ways — is way more interesting to me than lots o' close-ups. I want everything in motion, the Serenity crew, the camera, the story — so when it stops — say, to look out at Inara overlooking the mountains — we feel the stillness, we drink it.

The trick will always be to feel the thing without declaring it. This is an intimate epic. I want people to be too involved in the lives of our heroes to notice how epic it is, and too busy watching to see the beauty of the frame.

We might maybe wanna get Jack Green for this. Is he available?

I'm a guy who falls in love with the sound of my own pen. In TV, that's more acceptable, because generally speaking, you can sit down for five pages and yak it out. If the talk is interesting, you're doing fine. The question of momentum exists in TV, but in a movie, it's almost paramount. And then, very simply, I over-explained and I under-explained. And I knew this was going to happen; because I was so close to the material, I just didn't know where. And that's the part that when you're showing it to [a test] audience, 'Okay, we've told them five times this one thing. They get that. But they don't really get this other thing that we took for granted that it worked. So we have to trim some of this talk a bit, and then we need to add a line to strengthen this other concept that's not landing.' And I don't think I'd have as much of a problem with that on a film that didn't come with a history where I'm balancing the fans who have seen the show with the people who haven't, and trying to pay respect to both. But that sort of structuring the explanation has been a big change, [requiring] really questioning everything about it, so that I find pockets of air where I don't need it, so I can put it where I do — just a lot of things that obviously you do in TV as well, but really, really affect the rhythm of the thing in a movie.

You have to be a great deal more streamlined when you make a movie, because every piece of information that somebody is getting, they're getting for the first time. With TV, you have the luxury of assuming at some point that somebody already knows who these characters are. In a movie, you not only do not have that luxury, but everything that comes out of their mouths changes who they are significantly. The idea behind the movie is to destroy the notion of absolute good and evil and black and white — what some people consider 'sin,' I consider human characteristics. The worst people in the world might have the best ideas and the best intentions might create the worst monsters. That's basically the Operative, who embodies that in the movie in one person. But you're dealing with gray area in a movie that you still want people to get the feeling that [they] get from a movie that's [morally] black and white. You want to get that rousing feeling of, 'We want to fight back, we want to stand tall, we believe in these people.' And to get that in a world that is so hard is very tricky [laughs]. It's a high-wire act. I'm in the editing room today — I'm still on that wire.

Why did you decide to begin the film with Inara and Book already off the ship?

Because the movie explains itself as it goes along, because it's made for people who've never seen the show. In my first draft, I had Book on the ship and somebody — a new character that we didn't really care about — at Haven that Mal goes to for advice and that really didn't work in either way. Book didn't have enough to do and this other guy didn't matter. So that was kind of a two-fer. And with Inara, she had said in the series that she was going to leave the ship and she really didn't make sense on that ship. We had to come barreling in, and to explain someone whose agenda, like Book's, is not the same as the crew's means that it doesn't feel right, it doesn't feel mythic. It required more explanation than the movie had time for. And as in the series, she had said that she was going to get off anyway, it seemed like a perfect thing for Mal to have the woman he left behind, which is a noir thing, a Western thing, a romantic thing, it works in any genre. And it also works toward another end, which was that I

had to press 'reset' somewhat. When we left them [on *Firefly*], they really did seem to be one big happy family, with the exception of the fact that Inara was going to leave, because she was clearly way too much in love with Mal. So I needed to up the conflict, again, without being untrue to the audience that has seen the show.

How did you come to create the Operative [Chiwetel Ejiofor] as *Serenity*'s main villain?

The first thing the studio said to me was, 'We want someone famous to be the bad guy, because there's nobody famous in the movie.' Eventually, they changed their minds. They said, 'You know what? We don't have to go famous — just go for the best actor we can find.' Which I really appreciated. But they wanted [the Operative] to be, as they said, larger than life. So I had to figure out what I wanted to do with this guy. And I realized that what I wanted to do was the opposite of larger than life, which was to make him actual size, the least imposing person he could be. The gentlest, kindest, most thoughtful person who ever killed a bunch of people that there was. I came to this for a number of reasons. I have on occasion done movie montages with my wife, where I'll just throw up scenes on DVD or laser disc, one after another, in random order, just to delight her, and I said [while] struggling with writing the character, 'Okay, tonight, for my work, we're going to do a villain montage.' And I looked at a bunch of stuff. Ralph Fiennes in *Schindler's List*, Kenneth Branagh in *Othello*, Tim Roth in *Rob Roy* — even James Le Gros in *Living in Oblivion*, who is more of a buffoon than a true villain, but just sort of shook the mix up. The thing I came away with that really moved me was that all of these guys had this very strong conviction about who they were. I had Daniel Day-Lewis in *Gangs of New York*. Nobody has more conviction than Bill the Butcher. And that became the most interesting thing to me about my character. I realized that what I loved him for was that he's a better person than my hero. He's polite, he's open-minded, he cares about the future so much that he is willing to sacrifice his own soul to make a future better for other people. He literally does not believe that he is good enough to be in the world he wants to create. Now, the hero of traditionally a Western and many American films is always trying to create the world that can't include him: I think particularly of John Wayne in *The Searchers*. And that was a big role model for Mal, but at the same time, here is the Operative, who is somebody who wants a better world and will go to no end of horror to find it.

Mal is a person who believes very little and thinks he believes nothing, and is conflicted, often does terrible things, runs away for most of the movie, shoots not one but three unarmed men in the course of the film, and is kind of a despicable guy half the time, but he's the only person who can save us from ourselves. That's what makes the movie interesting to me. Writing the villain like that was hard, but once I landed on that, once I realized that this was a man who was terribly

polite and terribly self-effacing — self-effacing to the point of arrogance, humble to the point of arrogance, which again is an odd distinction, a sort of a paradox, but in fact, is the truth of the character, then he became not only easier to write but kind of lovely.

How did you decide to cast Chiwetel Ejiofor as the Operative?

It's funny. Chiwetel Ejiofor [pronounced CHEW-eh-tel EDGE-if-or] was absolutely the first name on every casting director's list. He had just done *Dirty Pretty Things*. I ended up going with Amy Britt [as *Serenity*'s casting director] , who had cast all my shows and had so brilliantly put together the cast of *Firefly*. And she was like every other casting director [in recommending Ejiofor], except that when she said his name, she actually pronounced it right, which I thought gave her points. And I saw him and I thought that he was wonderful, but [the studio executives] were talking about, 'Well, we want somebody who's someone more known.' And we went round and round. We had a lot of long lists and months and months of going over everything and Chiwetel came to America and I met with him and I found myself back right where we had started, thinking,

Above: The Operative (Chiwetel Ejiofor).

JOSS ON **LIGHT**

Initial musings...

Light. Light is good. It enables you to see things. Things that are in the movie. Lit-up movie things — that's what the public wants. Without light, all is emptiness. Or Radio, which is like emptiness but with talking and songs.

The universe is black. Light in space is hard, cold — no fill, no comfort. At least, it is in the documentaries. In our space, it's often coming from other sources: from Serenity itself, bouncing off passing moons or ships, from the proximity of atmosphere. We can play it how we want, soft, hard — according to the story's needs. But the light should have a reality to it, as with the lack of sound in space, that separates it from other films. Not always pretty, but always fresh.

Light on the ship comes from within. Put simply, it's the light of humans. Put less poetical, it's warm, lived in, textured and source-y. Seventies western — not to the extreme, it's a machine they're in, and not everything should be brown, but it's a good place to live — even with some dark patches.

The light here, too, must feel real — expressionistic in not being how we think of modern spaceships, not boringly bright, but it has to feel organic. I dislike heavily colored gels on ships. (And most places.) Maybe Mal is just trying to make his way between the dark patches, and maybe they seem to be closing in a little.

The light of **the school tent** is warm **and** cool, like an unhappy hostess's glazed smile. The light is bright, the colors rich but not gaudy. The outside of the tent is a few stops from being blown out, making the inside shady and comfortable by comparison. The only anomaly is River, who has the light of the computer screen bouncing under her, making her just slightly eerie. ('Cause I'm the first guy who ever did **that**.)

The Lab is the pale, dead green of a meat locker. It's clean, it's tidy, but it's an abattoir. And edges that also fall into shadow, to contrast the bright trust of the dream.

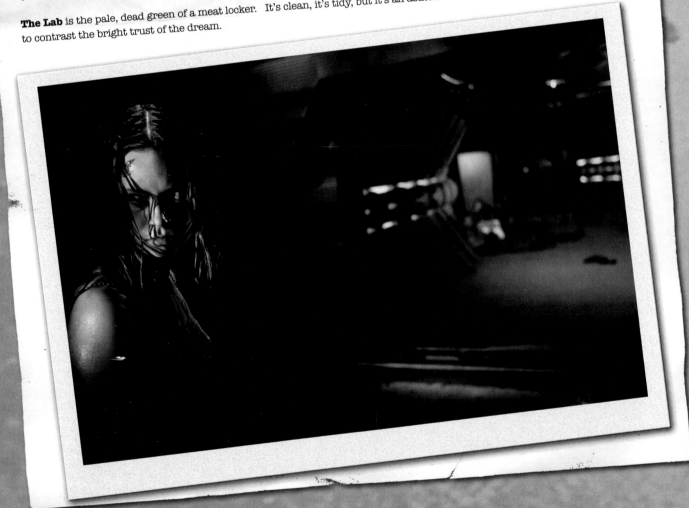

The records room introduces a man of discipline and integrity. It should be reserved. An unexpected line of dark red wood running up the hall... Standing out oddly like a single flower — a Japanese arrangement of a frame. The space must yet be connected to the Lab — it is after all the doctor's domain. Not overly warm.

The **companion training house** is lush. The light outside is not as bright as the school, not as demanding. The bright blue of the sky pops out against the deep reds and purples of the house, of Inara. We see her through water, behind screens... Inside the house is all fabric and shadow and mood. Patterns thrown through lace by light sometimes caressing her skin, sometimes an echo of her veils. This space is as romantic — again, with a gentle human simplicity — as we will encounter. Let her be our Ingrid Bergman, why the hell not? No fuzzy filters, though — I had a bad experience with one once.

If I could light **Mr. Universe** only with his screens and the glowing cords that run off them, I would.

Miranda is bright, hard-edged — uncomfortable. The shadows are straight and hit hard black. Possibly bleached a bit.

In London there's a lot of really bright, "70's modern" looking clubs, spare and fabulous and boxy and lime and cool orange. Architectural and often empty. A few steps away you'll find a pub — warm, lived-in, smoked-in, the dark brown wood of the booths, the inevitable picture of a hunt, or a sculling team, or a Queen... everything is nooks and hanging glasses and the dense roar of a comfortable crowd. And by the door: crass, endearingly strident "fruit machines" (the slot games), clashing with everything. **The Maidenhead** is a pub with a little bit of club. The bright, flat yellow of the automat gun locker interrupts the more intimate feel of the place, as does the corvue screen. Everything else comes from the tables — not in an eerie, underlit way and not in a shafty, spotlight way. Each booth should have the equivalent of a Chinese lantern on it. (It's very hard to say "Chinese Lantern" and not become Richard E. Grant in "The Player", but I'm trying.)

The light on their faces:

Mal is cragged, often shadowed, but strong, sad-eyed and kind.

Kaylee is round, warm, and open. Sexuality and honesty.

River is planed, underlit, eyes hooded. She's a question.

Simon works in angles as well, coolly handsome and hard to connect with — but ultimately he's a romantic.

Jayne doesn't give a good goddamn how he's lit.

Zoe glows. She cannot help it.

Wash is light, playful — often amongst his screens or slightly blown out by the sun of high atmosphere.

Book is solid, solid through.

Inara's light is complex, like Mal's. Hiding and beckoning.

Of course they're often all in the same general lighting and a lot of it is just how their faces read anyway, but there's your basic principles of facery for this crew.

So that means, what, Kinoflo? (I'm not entirely sure what a Kinoflo is, but I read about them all the time in American Cinematographer Magazine and I'm pretty sure mentioning one makes me sound all know-about-lightingy, which will garner respect. And I'd say it's working pretty good. The respect.)

I think that's enough for now. Sincerely, joss.

Above: Rehearsing Mal's climactic fight with the Operative.

'Did I just waste a really long time talking about different people, when I liked this guy from the start?' [laughs] If I could skip one process in filmmaking — and I can't — it would be casting. It's brutal, it's weird and it's exhausting. But Chiwetel came in and is delightful and interesting and energetic and fun and completely got the character and he brought me what I desperately needed, which is integrity. He has the most soulful eyes and when he speaks, you see so much decent, honest disappointment in the world for not being better than it is and I got just so much lovely stuff from him. It happened to be ironic that he was the name on everybody's lips, even if they mangled their lips in saying it, from the very start.

Obviously, Chiwetel and I had to do a lot of work, because his character is so undefined, he literally has no name, so [we worked on] how much aggression he was going to show and how much he was going to retire and to make people feel comfortable. [It] was a delicate dance we were doing. The one thing that [Ejiofor] asked — in the original script, we did not see him kill a certain character and he wanted to do it onscreen, because he wanted to show a moment of Mal having gotten to [the Operative], a moment of aggression that he himself didn't understand. It's in the movie — he violently stabs somebody and then looks like, 'That was odd.' And it really helps him sort of define his own arc.

Is there a difference in *writing* a hero and a villain when you're in the gray area?

Ultimately, yes, because your hero is going to do better things, sooner or later, than the villain does [laughs], and generally speaking, the villain's going to say something and then the hero is going to say something funnier.

***Serenity* incorporates Western, science-fiction, noir, horror …**

Yes, it absolutely evokes different genres. This is both my gift and my curse. I'm never satisfied with one genre. I never want to do one thing for two hours. Some people can, very compellingly, but the way I've described the future as being just bits of history mashed up — the movies I make are bits of genre mashed up. So are most movies. There are straight-up horror movie elements in *The Searchers*. Part of what I always want to evoke is, you don't know what movie you're in, you don't know where you are. Now Western is a big element of what I've done, and you can see it in some of the outfits and the desert and the bank that [the characters] rob. But it's not egregiously old-fashioned in that way, it's just making a statement — 'There's always going to be a frontier.' And when that frontier is space, we're still going to have very little to build with. There's still going to be rich and poor and there are still going to be people who are making do with what they've got. And that's a Western sensibility. My biggest problem when I was dealing with genre, and I've said this [elsewhere], 'I feel like Mal's in a Western and River's in a noir, and I'm not sure how to combine those.' My [Wesleyan University] professor Jeanine Basinger, to whom I often turn for advice, [said], 'Well, go to some of the Western noirs, like *Pursued* or *The Furies* or even *Johnny Guitar*.' In fact, there are a lot of Westerns that have a very noir feel to them. And you realize, oh, these two things aren't antithetical, or if they are, that's the point — they can exist in the same universe, so you can say, 'I will bring you out of a noir world, which is a small, cramped, dark, bleakly-lit world, into the Western world, which is a strong, wide, bright, comforting earthy world, where you do have, if not moral absolutes, a place to make a stand.'

The other thing I would say about genre is, I have discovered, watching [*Serenity*] with audiences, that I have what I refer to as kind of a Hong Kong sensibility. The first Hong Kong movie I ever saw was *Peking Opera Blues* and it remains one of my favorite movies. And the reason I loved it so and the reason I love the early John Woo flicks was because you never actually knew what scene you were in. There is a convention in American cinema to fall back on clichés — or on time-honored structure — so much that you always know exactly what scene you're in. And in these [Hong Kong] films, where you thought you were going to be terrified, the broadest comedy might appear. Whenever you thought this guy has been defeated, he might suddenly come back and kill everybody in the room and *then* suddenly be defeated. You just never knew. The scales were always tipping and the genres were always mixing, and they were having a great time and so was I. I find that American audiences who are not used to my work — because I did that in *Buffy* and *Angel* all the time — have a harder time with it. Part of this high-wire act has been also to work the rhythms of the movie so that people were not upset by the shifts, so that you could have the relationship between Mal and Inara, which is basically a '30s romantic comedy relationship, pop up in the middle of my Western noir, and then do *Dawn of the Dead* [with the Reavers]. Because, again, all of these genres have enough in common — *Dawn of the Dead* is *Zulu* is *The Magnificent Seven* is *Seven Samurai*. The siege movie is not limited to zombies. [With the Reavers], I was trying to evoke horror and the horror movie.

Was there discussion on exactly *how* horrific the Reavers would look?

The make-up was very tricky. I wanted something that was grotesque, but not gratuitously. The movie must be a PG-13 movie, and yet the Reavers are supposed to have done horrible things to themselves and luckily, as in any good horror or siege movie, the less you see, the better, so I was able to do some things that were just

appalling, but only for a flash, and then some thing that were a little more palatable for the longer takes. I literally had, 'Okay, this is my hero [close-up] make-up, because I can look at this guy, and this is my background make-up, because this guy is just so scary.'

Were there Reaver make-ups that, if you had brought them closer to the camera and/or lingered on them longer, would have jeopardized the PG-13 rating?

WHEDON [laughs]: I already have [jeopardized the PG-13 rating] and we're in the process of working that out. It's not a very bloody film, but there's some blood. Actually, there's a lot of stabbing. Most of it's off-screen, but it needs to be handled tastefully. This is a bit of back and forth that I've always had in my work. I'm not interested in gore, but I'm always interested in making things as difficult for my heroes as possible. So they really get the shit kicked out of them.

I wanted to just say on the subject of blood, Camille [Calvet], our head of make-up, was doing Mal's make-up at the end of the fight and he was just covered head to toe in blood. And I [said], 'Okay, sweetie, we have to pull this back. I want to see that he's suffered, but this isn't *Sorority House Massacre*.' And she looked at me: 'Oh, my God! Did you know? That [*Sorority House Massacre*] was my first film!' And I was like, 'I didn't even know it was a real movie!'

Was there a deliberate decision not to use horses in the movie?

No. It was like, 'Whoa, I forgot something, and I think it whinnies.' I didn't see a place for them. Fox was very uncomfortable with the Western elements of the [TV] show. Universal didn't have that mandate, they didn't mind that — I mean, they didn't want obviously something that looked like a stupid pastiche, but they'd have no problem with a horse if it felt endemic, if it felt natural.

Below: The director, directing.

Did working with the various production departments shape *Serenity* in any way?

A props designer is going to show you something that makes you go, 'You know what? That's a perfect example of how these [characters] jerry-rig things together' and a costume designer is going to show you an aspect of a character that you hadn't seen, like Gina's unbelievably pumped arms [laughs]. In some departments, I looked for more vision, and in some, I found it unexpectedly. Every department affects other ones. You can learn about character from a stunt coordinator, production designer, from anybody — through environment. Especially when you're creating worlds. There is no world in this movie that we ourselves have stepped on [in real life], but they all have to feel familiar. So when you're creating worlds like that, inevitably, the surroundings, costumes, props, the lighting, they're all going to inform character in ways you might not have seen coming.

***Serenity* costume designer Ruth Carter has said that you told her of the wardrobe items, 'If this says just one thing, it's wrong ...'**

Yes. We always set out to make more than one statement, because one statement is the past. And the future is, like I said, the past in a blender. Costume-wise, that

was very important. Inara had a very Indian aesthetic, but we couldn't just go with an Indian look — that would be a disservice, it would be cheap. And we also didn't have giant dollars to create enormous costumes and Inara was always the trickiest, because she was the one who had a wardrobe on that ship, so it was always a question of mixing and matching, which is actually enormous fun if you love wardrobe, and I confess that I do.

How long did it take to devise the opening sequence, which goes through several different layers of time, location and reality?

Actually, not that long. The structure of the pre-credits sequence came rather quickly, and was charming to me because it is constantly discombobulating and re-evaluating itself. It's been somewhat less charming to certain audiences. The tricks of going from what appears to be narration to a classroom that turns out to be a dream sequence that turns out to be a hologram, all of that reassessing of where we are is meant to sort of make the audience uncomfortable and not trust what they're seeing because that's the state that River's in.

Then when we get to [the ship] Serenity, things calm right down and become linear, because Serenity has a sweetness to it, a comfort; even if it's not the stablest of homes, it *is* home. So that just sort of felt right to me. And I love not knowing where I am. Not in a sense of, 'Well, now I'm confused,' but in a sense of, 'Oh, I've made an assumption and it's been pulled out from under me, and the moment it is pulled out from under me, I understand that.'

How did you create the shot of the Operative walking through River's hologram?

Through many, many, many versions sent to us by the CGI house. [Ejiofor and Glau] were in front of a green screen and then he just walked through the space in front of the green screen and we put the background behind both of them and the CGI house worked on different ways that he could interact with that. The idea of it was very simple — I wanted him to come through River's face, their eyes in exactly the same place, to make a connection between them, because his whole mission is finding her. I spent a lot of time trying to show Chiwetel the straightest walk a person could do so that he didn't go from side to side, which reads in that close a shot as hugely jogging. The physical logistics of the thing are tough, but the effects houses are usually able to tweak them if there's a problem.

Is there something different in the way Serenity is introduced that tells us, 'Okay, we're out of the holograms now, don't expect a further pull-back'?

Well, yes. When we suddenly cut to black at the end of the pre-credits sequence, right before the word 'Serenity' comes on, we go into the two longest shots in the movie: the first being the exterior of the ship and the second being a four-and-a-half-minute oner [single tracking shot] that takes us all the way through the ship and meets every character on the ship and sees every room in the ship in one shot. And this, again, was deliberately to say, 'Okay, we're done messing with you. River has a fractured mind, but this is a solid place that she has come to.' I've often referred to *Serenity* as Mal's story as told by River. [River] comes at things sideways, the way the story does. But once Mal is introduced, there is more of a comfort. I deliberately went through every room in the ship and met everybody in one shot not to show off camerawork — in fact, a lot of people saw that and didn't know it was a oner, which is the best compliment that could be given — but because what I wanted was a sense of community and continuity and a sense of safety, and to give things not a theatrical but kind of a humanistic feel, so that everybody has a chance to interact and it's all happening in front of you and it's not cut up, it's sort of written in stone. *Mr. Rogers* is very popular with younger kids, because he does no cutting — he takes you from place to place with him everywhere he goes, and that's one of the reasons why it's so soothing. Well, not that I need to soothe the audience, and not that they're little children, but I think something can be said for long

takes, when people are watching people in a space that they understand, even subconsciously, it's actually there and people are actually interacting in that time and space. Even though the ship is not in great shape, the safety of, 'I am staying with these people and they're not going to leave me behind, they're not going to abruptly change my view. In fact, we're going to be with them the whole way. And even though Mal is getting in Simon's face and saying mean things, what I'm getting as an audience member about this place is that it has structure, it has a lived-in feel, I understand the space I'm in for the first time in the movie.' And that speaks to the great contradiction in Mal. He thinks that he's a heartless badass, and the movie is really about him finding out that, in fact, he's not.

Because I introduced Serenity in the big oner, I introduced everybody all at once in a very dispassionate fashion, and the problem became, people are very identified with River at the beginning of the movie — they don't know that Mal is the guy to watch. I thought that because we follow him through the whole oner that people would identify with him, but he's kind of putting us off, staying away from us, the camera, being mean to Simon and people don't know this is their guy. When I looked at the [rough cut], I saw what's missing emotionally is [Mal and River's] connection and I need just one tiny privileged moment between the two of them early on. I needed to tell the audience about Mal, and so I added one little scene that we shot on a Sunday, literally a one shot in the cargo bay that was focusing on Mal for a moment and River coming up to him and kind of handing him the movie, kind of saying, 'I'm watching *you*,' so that the audience would get, 'Okay, this guy's emotional journey is going to be something to keep our eyes on, because this girl is watching him and she's our intro into this.'

Was designing the tracking shot that introduces Serenity and the crew a huge design/logistics challenge?

WHEDON: Well, that's the good thing about being the writer/director. I knew exactly where I wanted the camera to be while I wrote the scene. For example, I knew exactly which wall had to fly [be movable] so that we could step onto a crane and go up to the cat-walk so that we could see River at the end of the shot, and I knew that before the script was finished.

What it really was, was me learning about the kind of prep [preparation] I needed to do. We had rehearsed for two weeks, which was very new to me. I'd never had any more than a read-through, with the exception of the creation of Illyria [on *Angel*], since I'd started [as a director]. I thought at first that I wasn't going to need that kind of rehearsal time. When we got to the oner [long single take], I realized I could have used another week. Because I was so used to everybody being locked into their characters that I didn't really give them that much direction, because it seemed sort of a no-brainer, but the fact is, in a movie, it's different. Everything needs to be worked and fine-tuned, so when we got the camera up and ready and everything set and all the lighting and all the stuff I thought was going to take forever, we got in and I realized I had a lot more work to do with the actors than I had done. And it was just one of those lessons about everything in a movie is going to matter a little bit more. Nothing can be left to chance.

The first half [of the shot] took thirty takes and the second half took sixteen, because you have so many factors, but we were ready for it production-wise. And actually, the cameraman, Mark Moore, the Steadicam operator and our first camera operator, misstepped once. Which, considering how much of that he was doing on stairs backwards, was pretty extraordinary.

The Steadicam operator didn't fall backwards down the stairs ...?

No, nothing like that. He's fine. He took one wrong step, bumped the camera — in a total of forty-five takes.

What does the added rehearsal time of the feature film schedule provide?

You can really hone something so that you understand it better, so that you come at it through all levels, and I absolutely had the actors play off each other and give me insight into what I had written that I did not know was there. At the same time, you'll find in rehearsal, 'You know what? This really could play out a couple different ways, camera-wise or in terms of levels. How angry do we want to be here, how scared? Let's go ahead knowing that we're going to shoot some choices.' This was particularly the case with Chiwetel, because his character is again such a contradiction. Whether he's being menacing or whether he's being the politest man in the world, or whether he's actually angry or whether he's just doing his job, these were things that on the day, we said, 'Okay, let's try a couple of options.'

Do you direct action sequences differently than you direct dramatic sequences?

It sort of depends on what it is you're doing. One of the things you have to be careful about is to make sure that it sure doesn't *feel* different for an audience, that you have the same kinetic energy and the same kind of style going in a dialogue scene that you have in an action scene. The same goes for CGI. Obviously, it's different in the sense of amount of prep it takes and it's different because everything has to be done for maximum impact. I never actually enjoyed directing action [for episodic TV], simply because I never had time to really get into it. [On *Serenity*], it's different because I do have the time to get into it, so I can take the time to have the fun to set up stunts and I'm very hands-on about figuring out gags during stunts and working with what I have. [Filming action] provides you with choices, but it also provides you in a way with fewer [options]. If somebody is faking hitting somebody, you really only have two places you can put the camera, on either side of either of them, where it looks like they're actually getting hit.

In this case, directing the action was definitely fun, because my actors actually did ninety-five percent of the action. Almost all of the [main characters'] action work, with the exception of a few wire gags, are done by my actors. Nathan and Chiwetel beat the thundering heck out of each other. And not being stuntmen, they didn't always miss. Which was *great* for the film. Nathan threw himself face-first on the ground for six takes before I realized that's what he was doing. I thought he was just selling it, and then his face started to puff up on one side. I was like, 'Oh, okay, no Take Seven ...'

Summer trained for months before we started shooting. I hired Summer at first because she was a ballet dancer. And knowing she was a ballet dancer meant she was an athlete and she was limber, and given the right coaches, she could probably work her way through a fight better than most action stars. She proved me right, and I love to be right. She worked with our stunt coordinator Chad [Stahelski] and his second, Hiro [Koda], for all those months, re-learning how to position herself from a ballet structure to a martial arts structure, which is very different physically. And then I had the benefit of an actress who could not only kick somebody in the very tippy-top of their head, but keep on doing it continuously. She learned the fights as though they were dances, which meant two things. It meant that I was able to do long takes, which to me is the most gratifying thing in the world. Right now, everything is about slo-mo, it's about cut-cut-cut, it's about sort of the effect over the reality of the thing. Nowadays, anybody can do anything [on film], but none of it feels real, none of it feels like it's actually happening. One of the things about *Firefly* is that it's supposed to be grounded in a sort of hard-scrabble reality. And everything that my actors were doing was actually happening and some of the things that Summer was doing were just remarkable.

The other thing about Summer being an athlete was, Take Eleven — faster than Take One. And that's not something I'm used to. But I learned that, for example, when we were shooting, she tagged a guy, meaning that she hit him by mistake when she was doing one of her kicks. And [stunt coordinator] Chad came up to me beaming: 'Okay, now she's going to really start to go. She tagged a guy. That means she knows exactly how far she can kick. Which means she knows exactly what those limitations are, so she's not going to be scared any more.' And in fact, she sped up and sped up and sped up, because she got more and more comfortable with the dance. So some of the stuff we put on film I think is really lovely, because we had the time to prep, we had the opportunity to really do something epic and then absolutely shoot it as though it were anything but epic, shoot it as though it just happened to be happening, so that it didn't get so full of itself that you expected people to be leaping thirty feet in the air, which cannot happen in my movie.

Is the bar fight an homage to any particular movie Western bar brawl, or were you actually trying to avoid doing things we've seen in previous Western fights?

I definitely tried to avoid Western clichés. I said, 'You know what? If that guy fell on a table, the table wouldn't smash in half. They build tables better than that.

Above: The highly trained River Tam, played by Summer Glau, an actress who can 'kick somebody in the very tippy-top of their head'.

JOSS ON **MUSIC**

500 years from now, the Beatles will still be remembered, though they will often be misspelled. Beyond that, all bets are off.

In the central planets, everybody has access to everything. We don't live there. We live on the outer planets, where the entertainment you have, you make. The first thing a person in the wilderness can make to separate himself from the base and wooly beasts is a joke. The second is music. We make it with what we can carry. Working, primarily, up: Voice. Drum. Blowing air through wood. Guitar.

The future is made up of the past. The past in a Cuisinart, but the past none-the-less. Stories are made of other stories, picked apart, packed together, personalized, plagiarized (but let's not stress that last part.) Culture is made of what we already understand mixed with what we newly embrace. We go back, we go forwards. This story is a western. This world is science fiction. This movie is an epic. But stripped bare, rubbed raw. It hasn't the comfort or pomp of an old-school epic. Or the distancing strangeness of much great science fiction. Or horses. Everything it is, it hides. I'm gonna be saying this till your ears bleed: Contradictions. Hiding. A bigger than life tale doing everything in its power to look actual size.

Star Wars was balls to the wall Big Show, and the music was like the Force: it surrounds you, binds you, comforts you like Alec's Obi-wan voice. Separates good from evil and happy from sad and makes damn sure every climax hits you right in the THX (which did not actually exist when Star Wars came out — it was, come to think of it, CAUSED by Star Wars.) **The Matrix** brought the modern world to the modern world, slammin' techno for eye-popping visuals (that soon became as repetitive as, say, slammin' techno.) Now there's us, staking out our piece of cinematic turf (might be small, but it's ours). And the music has to fit the vision as specifically as it did for those films. OUR music comes from THEIR music, this scrappled bunch. It is spare, intimate, mournful and indefatigable. Strength comes from pain, hope from the understanding of despair. Serenity (the ship, not the movie) (or the valley) is a tiny light in a vast blackness. Space isn't filled with the Force, or even Jerry Goldsmith's Federation marches — fellah, space isn't filled with anything. That's why it's called "space". Which makes the fact that the first time I hear music in this film is in space a little ironic. But we'll get to that.

Let's get specific. This is a science fiction western noir action suspense drama. (Yes, another one of those.) Its roots are in the western film and in the history of the west (two remarkably different things). Our people are pioneers. Their landscape is dry, dusty. Their vernacular draws from the west, their instrumentation does too. Jayne has a guitar, which he occasionally plucks at. It's hard for me not to think of a fiddle sawing defiantly when I watch this ship go. But this is not a tale of the old west, and

to step **too** far into that vernacular would cause justified derision. (Let alone the fact that a lot of the 'old-west'erners were Eastern Europeans.) So what else have we got? Culturally, there is a flush of Chinese in our white-trash culture, and that works out easily — your basic pentatonic scale evokes China as much as it does old-timey country. Eastern scale patterns inevitably hit blue notes and minor threads and that's what makes a melody stick. (Hope from despair, see. Hope without despair is John Phillips Souza — it makes your teeth ache.) Embracing the cultural blenderizing also allows for a whole bunch of interesting instrumentation. But mixed up, hidden, or it's as much a cliché as the western feel. We don't want to be too specific about culture or time. We want to be comfortable enough with the sounds not to let them take us out of the story, but not so comfortable that we begin to be told where the story is. Tricksome.

As before: Voice, drum, wind, and string.

Voice is a lovely and unexpected instrument, but right now there are two voices in Hollywood: that middle eastern wailin' gal that works in **Troy**, **Black Hawk Down** and any movie that takes place east of Rhode Island, or that Irish chick who sounds like (and usually is) Enya. I think you get both in **Gladiator**. (For the price of one!) So for voice, those are the pitfalls to avoid right now.

Drum works wonders, used right. Can do the work of an orchestra, and everything in the world sounds different from everything else when you hit it. (I have tested this on all my assistants.)

Wind — dangerous. I just hate flutes. Hate them. I love a bassoon or an Oboe better than fine wine and I would love to find a place for a harmonica that didn't scream either "civil war" or "Neil Young Song". (Not that there's anything wrong with a Neil Young song. Don't ever be dissin' the Neil.) But wind instruments are either too airy or too sophisticated to feel like my bunch, so moderation is a watchword.

Strings. Guitar. One will appear, so that's no stretch. And folks could lug a fiddle farther than just about any instrument. But they walk the line with the obvious western cliché problem, so the melodies will have to compensate. Cellos are just cool, there's nothing to be done about it. Bouzoukis — I'm really not sure how to spell them, so let's just move on. Sitar's like the harmonica — if you can hide it, it's a powerful tool. If you can't, it's only one thing.

Nothing here can be only one thing. Nothing can be that specific about era or culture. Our conceit is that after hundreds of years of musical evolution, things have been pared down rather than built up. Is there room for the Big Show or the techno or the Beatles or whatever's next in pop culture? Everyone's invited. In pieces. Grafted to a very simple mandate: Life is simple in structure, complex in tone. Structure: we have to eat, make money, avoid firey death. Tone: we are not the good guys. There is no death star, no total victory, no easy decisions. And way too much fiery death.

Let's get **less** specific. In fact, let's make a grand and sweeping statement. This movie will have less score, and a simpler score, and more hidden workings in music and sound design, than its epic action might indicate. A documentary — a "found" movie. Unpolished. And because I live for contradictions, let's make another grand sweeper: This movie will have more score than I think it will. Because it IS an action movie, and some of that action will be in space, where there is no sound BUT music, and the score will have to do some double-time. And 'cause every now and then, I just wanna break someone's heart.

Now let's get disgustingly specific. Let's go through the story.

The cold open: River's escape and the introduction of the Operative. I hear no music here (save possibly for the Op's entrance, if he wants for a theme) unless it's low, discordant — the distant clanging of metal and low strains run backwards, unsettling, more sound than music, until the sound is (as scripted) sucked out of the screen and we go to black, thence to:

The title. The ship. This is the first time I hear clear, pure music, and it's her theme, Serenity's. A violin, or two voices oddly harmonized, or something I haven't thought of yet but what it says is "Home." Not safe harbor, but a place you wanna hang.

Once we're on the ship, on the job, in the bank, I don't hear anything. I don't hear anything until the Reavers come, and then it hits hard and I don't think of it as music, I think of it as "get those guys away from me". Banging on a can, a fiddle scratched taut at its highest register — nothing so comforting as an orchestra, but room for a very tense ensemble.

Back on the ship — Mal's contemplation of Inara's picture might draw in a simple theme — they are, after all, in love. Thwarted love, the bestest kind. And Kaylee's wistfulness carries over to an image of Inara herself, one with no sound, so I feel like this theme might come through to the scene with Sheydra.

Beaumonde is full of music, both live and recorded. Let's figure out what pop songs will sound like in 500 years! It'll be easy! And in the cacophony of the competing sounds, no one will notice we failed!

River's little "episode": I've described this in stunt meetings as "**Robert Altman's THE MATRIX**". Which is to say, no slo-mo, no impossible gags, and all the messiness of fifteen guys trying to either fight or run away from this lithe little

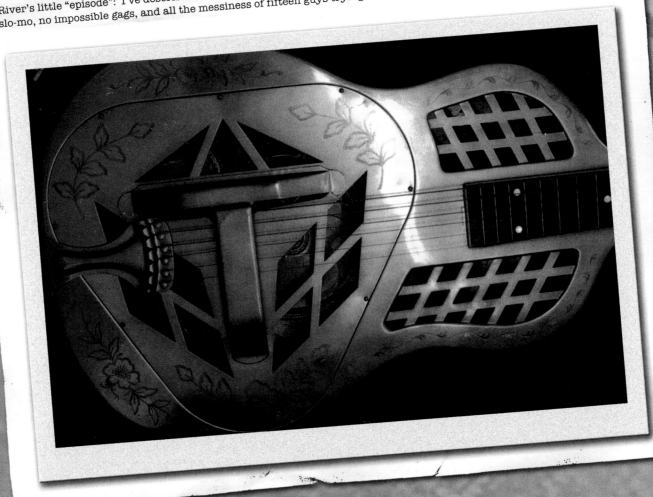

killer. Here, music should creep in, so we're too busy gaping to notice it but building enough so that when Mal and River point their guns at each other it can STOP — and stop us with it.

The Operative again, looking at images of River, of Mal, of Inara. Do we hear their themes here, or should we wait?

River in the storage locker: she's got a lot to go through here, awake and asleep. And she is the narrator of this film, which is just one more reason to take the rustic aesthetic of the music and filter it through a modern — and odd — perspective. Her theme is plaintive, unwelcoming but heartfelt. She is the monster. She is the damsel. She is the action hero. She's from the central planets, where the Asian influence is more keenly felt. (She happens to look Asian, or Slavic, when she is in fact a Texan.) She is a beating heart and a worried mind. Her (later) dreams are a horror, where the music actually outweighs the narrative — what the hell is so scary about people taking a nap?

The night scene at Shepherd Book's: Jayne sits by the fire and provides a gentle, almost-bluesy underscoring to the intimate scene, and he provides it a week from Sunday, so we better get on that.

Mal and Inara on the vidscreens: No music. Let's let them be uncomfortable.

Mal and the Operative: again, the Operative would never be so crass as to enter with music. It would come with the fight, and carry through the retreat to the ship.

Mal's confusion, River's escape: some hits in here, keep the momentum up.

The return to Book's: it comes as we enter, highlights Kaylee's finding the boy, but Book's scene with Mal should play without it — there is no comfort here. He's not going into the light.

The reaverized ship: So there's music here. Things are getting hairy. And soon after, sad and romantic, what with Mal and Inara and all. And when the group gathers to see the Reaver armada... Well, I think the music builds on all their faces and then disappears when we see the Armada. The scope of it. Here is true emptiness. The music comes back when that spotlight washes over them, following them... tense and quiet. This is a horrible place to be. (Take "The Hills Have Eyes" and put a submarine in it.) (Wait a minute, I smell franchise...)

Miranda: again, it is still and sterile, so the music comes in ambient waves, never settling. Then it hits you with the corpses, and River's freakout takes us deep into it — and keeps us there all the way through Dr Caron's speech. The core of the movie is in here. The Very Worst. It should be tragic, because of this woman's misguided decency, but also because the revelation frees River's mind and allows it to cohere to the point of accepting and codifying actual tragedy; the comfort of simple, genuine sadness. It even gets Mal and Inara to talk plainly for the first time in their lives. There's beauty in it.

Mal' St. Crispin's Day speech: Oh come on. Of course.

The Air War: As mentioned before, no sound in space, so I'm assuming we need a broad sound here. This is one of the few (actually, two) places I think we might need an orchestra — but I could be wrong.

The Siege: Here's the other place I feel a full sound, just to evoke the elegiac nature of our heroes' sacrifice, and offset the horror of the Dawn of the Dead-style massacre they're getting into. (This is only partially about ratings.) Then it's action-o-rama. Mal vs. the Operative may carry some of the siege over into it. At this point, we're in it, and we can worry less about hiding it. The music can be bigger because the cause is bigger. WE are bigger, or as the Simpsons would say, we are embiggened.

The funeral/rebuilding montage: all music, but definitely our old accustomed sound, spare and lovely.

The end: Oh, we'll build, but we'll cut out fast when the ship starts falling apart again.

The End Credits: Here's where you take a theme from the movie and have someone sing over it so you can have a pop hit! I'm as excited as anyone. I like Tsuji Ayano for this. She plays the Ukulele and only sings in Japanese, but she's totally adorable and I'm pretty sure Bryan Adams is busy. (Actually, the only time I remember actually liking this trick is David Sylvan singing over Ryuichi Sakamoto's indelibly brilliant score for **Merry Christmas Mister Lawrence**. But I liked it pretty well then.)

I think that's enough for now. I am drawn, in post script, to the parallel between the four instruments I've highlighted and the four themes from **Once Upon a Time in the West**. Morricone announced everyone operatically, which we will never do (or admit to doing) but the elements, the voice, harmonica, guitar, percussion, are so prevalent. I guess they're both Fairy Tales, in a way. I like the connection. It's in there, like everything else, hidden. Always hidden.

So let's avoid that.' There is a Western cliché — or I should say a Western moment — in the bar, but it is, I think, in the spirit of *Serenity*. Very simply, when [River] comes near the bar, it automatically closes down. You see metal partitions going up or down everywhere the bar is, and that to me is a futuristic version of the bartender taking down the mirror because there's a brawl in his bar.

How do you work with the stunt coordinator on set in terms of directing stunt sequences?

I always have the stunt coordinator give the commands if he wants to, because he is creating what is more importantly than anything else a safe space, and he has a rapport with his people and the stuntmen who are in that bar scene or the actors. When it comes to setting a frame [deciding where the camera should be], I'll always take his suggestion, but I'm completely in charge of that. If I'm looking for something in the performance during the fight, I'll [give those directions]. But when it comes to rolling and setting the scene in motion, that belongs to the stunt coordinator and I'm very wary of getting in the way of that.

Did you have an overview of what should be done as CGI [computer-generated imagery] and what you felt had to be done as "practical" on-set filming?

I did. We did the "Mule" chase, where [Mal, Jayne, Zoe and River] are in a convertible hovercraft and being chased by Reavers, and I absolutely demanded that we shoot everything with the actors physically on location. We built different rigs to accomplish that: a rig that could turn, a rig that could be towed from the side, a rig that could be towed from behind, a rig for long shots — everything so I could shoot as much practically as possible. Now, ultimately, I ended up needing to have CGI [for the sequence]. I always knew we would, but I ended up needing to have more than I'd hoped [laughs] and wishing I'd shot more [practically] than I did. I suppose that's the curse of most directors. [With CGI], you have a lot more opportunity to make it better when you've blown it, which is nice. But I [felt] very strongly, 'If we do this chase and our close-ups are in front of a green screen or we're using digital doubles, at best, it'll look just slightly off, and at worst, it'll look like *Catwoman*.' Because it's very important to me that people believe what they're seeing, that they believe the veracity of this tale and these people, I wanted everything to be as practical as possible and when the CGI is used, to mix it with practical as often as possible, so that you would never get that airless feeling of something that has just been completely designed inside a cubicle.

That's something that Zoic [the CGI effects company that did the effects on *Firefly* and *Serenity*, supervised by Loni Peristere] brought to the table in the show that had really never been seen before, which was CGI that felt homemade, handheld, finding the zoom, hitting a flare ... CGI was always the cleanest thing in a movie and they really went out of their way to dirty it up. But at the same

Left: Joss Whedon watches playback of a take, as Adam Baldwin looks on.

time, and I learned more about this in post[-production on *Serenity*] than I had in all my years doing TV, [with CGI] you have to block things out as specifically and as carefully as you do if they were real, as if they were physically in front of you, and you have to make sure the camera is in exactly the right place, because you're still doing the same thing, you're telling the story.

Regarding the function of Mr. Universe [David Krumholz] in the storyline, do you believe a government really can be shamed into or out of what it's doing by the actions of individuals?

Ultimately I think we say in the film, people's eyes have been opened up, there is a scandal — we don't know if it's going to change anything. We don't know if that's going to cause a change in the government — it's certainly not going to make the Alliance leave the occupied independent planets, it's not going to destroy the concept [of the Alliance], which by the way I don't think it should, because the Alliance is in theory something great, but — and this is the way I tended to end episodes of television, too — unless you're doing a '70s movie, you don't want it to end miserably, but you also don't want to wrap everything up with a neat little bow. In an episode, if I had somebody who was traumatized, for example, 'Earshot,' the episode of *Buffy* with [Jonathan, played by Danny Strong] who's going to kill himself with the gun, we didn't end going, 'And now he's fine.' We ended the episode with, 'He needs a lot of help and he's been kicked out of school because he had a gun and the guy is a mess, but he's not trying to kill himself, so a step has been taken.' That's the way to end something, so you understand there is positive resolve and you might not necessarily need to see the rest of it, but it ain't all sunshine and roses. And that's the same with *Serenity*. The idea was to say people can make a difference, they can show the wrongs that are being done, they can speak out against them and make people aware of them. They can even create giant scandals. Sometimes they can topple governments; sometimes they can't make a dent. The point is always that the truth is more important than the power structure, and whether you make a dent or not, the fact that you succeeded in trying is a victory.

In the *Angel* episode "A Hole in the World," which you wrote and directed, the characters get into a monumental argument over who would win in a fight, astronauts or cavemen. Does the conflict between the Serenity crew and the Reavers constitute an answer to that argument?

[Laughs] You know, I would say, the Reavers aren't in that argument. The cavemen vs. astronauts would definitely be Serenity vs. the Alliance. When Fred said [on *Angel*], 'Cavemen win,' it was the most depressing thing imaginable. And *Serenity* is kind of an answer to it that says, 'Well, there's a *reason* why the astronauts shouldn't win.' Mal's a throwback. The Operative says as much and he's quite right. Mal's the kind of person that shouldn't be in a perfect world, and he's the kind of person who will save us from the concept of a perfect world.

As you're hoping to continue the *Serenity* universe, was there a question of 'Who can I least afford to lose,' in terms of certain dramatic plot developments toward the finale?

You know, my original intent was that you never leave a man behind. Or a woman, or anyone. Dramatically, the more I worked on [the screenplay], the more it became clear that in order to make people feel that this was real, a certain shocking thing is going to have to happen. I've only ever seen one movie where the stakes were high and there's a siege and you're really engaged, and absolutely nobody dies that you care about — *Zulu* managed to get away with everything, including Michael Caine's lovely light blue eye shadow. When you have an ensemble, you think about what people are going to take away with them at the end of the movie, and you don't think about the second movie until you've made the first one. And that's just a very strict rule with me. By the way, there's a strong possibility that everybody would return for a sequel. How is that possible? Not my usual way — there are no amulets to be had for love or money. But there's every chance you could see these characters again. But the fact is, my first draft was two hundred pages long. It was basically like I wrote Season Two [of *Firefly*]. And then I was like, 'Okay, that's great, now turn it into a movie.' And you have to up the stakes, you have to make it real, you have to make it matter, and you cannot let your hope for a sequel guide what you're going to do in a movie, because it will lessen the chance that there will *be* one.

Do you have a single favorite line of dialogue?

You know, when we're editing, I always say, 'That's my favorite line.' And I don't remember when I say it. A lot of them are cut, because beloved though they may have been, they're either unclear or unnecessary. The one that I'm going to point out is Jewel's line: 'And don't fly in anything with a Capissen Thirty-Eight engine, they fall right out of the sky.' I just think it flowed beautifully and she just nailed it, gave it all the emotion and just made it just adorable. It's possibly my favorite delivery.

Do you have a favorite moment in *Serenity*?

My favorite moment came from Nathan and Morena, when we were talking about the comm video, where [Inara] invites [Mal] to come and it's a trap. I had added a line about stuff in a trunk, because she needed to have a weapon and that weapon used to be a bow and arrow. When the movie comes out, it will be a cool gun that is fired, much as though you were holding a bow and arrow, that will be CGI'ed over the [originally filmed] bow and arrow that the audience didn't buy at all. Such are the vagaries of filmmaking. But I had to invent the necessity for her to be able to change clothes into something a little more fighter-y and to have something to fight with that was not a machine gun — that's not Inara's way. So I added what I thought was a very clumsy piece of writing about a

trunk. [Mal] says, 'You left some of your stuff in a trunk and I didn't look through the stuff' and they play a very sweet moment there, but I actually ended up going back and writing a bit more about it because Nathan said to me, 'You know I looked through all that stuff. I've smelled that stuff.' And Morena separately said, 'You know I left that trunk on purpose, that has all my best-smelling stuff, so that he wouldn't be able to forget.' And they had both completely internalized and made useful what to me was something very clunky and made it very beautiful, and then it became a great moment between them, where they're both, 'Ahh, ahh, ahh, I didn't ...' 'Well, I didn't ...' 'Well, I certainly didn't ...' And it's clear that that thing represents the fact that neither of them has let go of each other, which, when I had written, it wasn't there.

Adam [as Jayne] — this man brings more questions and more business than anybody south of Tony Head [Giles on *Buffy*]. He wanted to give Shepherd Book cigars. [Observing that the script says], 'Shepherd Book is smoking a cigar,' [Baldwin asked], 'Can I bring him a cigar as a present and then can I be smoking that cigar [later], because I'm thinking about Shepherd Book.' Every scene, he had five things that he'd like to incorporate or be doing.

I also loved, in a very different way, the moment where Gina said to me, 'Now, this scene where [Mal] says at the end, "Do you think she'll hold together?" and I say, "She's tore up plenty, but she'll fly true" about Serenity, obviously, this scene is about me.' And I said, 'Obviously.' And Nathan looked up and said, 'What? It is?' Nathan has paragraphs and paragraphs about every line and every scene and his perspective on things that everybody's doing — he absolutely didn't get that at all and [then said], 'Oh, God, that's so obvious!' That cracked me up. It was just an extraordinary process for me, because learning about your own screenplay from the actors is so gratifying. It means they're invested, it means they're intelligent, it means there are layers there that you get. And when it's bigger than you are, that's what makes it art.

Did you have a scene that was your favorite in terms of the experience of shooting it?

Probably the first thing that comes to mind — the funeral, because it was the first day for a lot of people, and it's the farthest out we ever went [on location], and we shot it with no sound, three times, in the space of about an hour, because the sun was setting. We shot it twice before the sun set and then at the insistence of [director of photography] Jack Green, we shot at some point after the sunset. It was magic hour and I [thought], 'Well, the sun was hitting them, it was so dramatic and beautiful and this is washed-out, but we'll do a quick version of this, because it's Jack and I respect him and maybe I'll see something

Above: Morena Baccarin and Nathan Fillion brought their own perspective to Mal and Inara's relationship.

Above: 'Miranda.' Shooting the moment when River looks up at the screen in the Maidenhead bar.

that I'm not getting.' And the only stuff we used [in the film] was from the third time we shot it, Jack's time. It's the most beautiful colors and skin tones and feeling I've ever seen. And the feeling we all had that day was really exciting.

I'd also say, the scene between Simon and River in the storage locker, because the storage locker was the first stuff we shot on [the film set for the ship] Serenity. Stepping back on board Serenity was extremely moving. Nathan came up and he said, 'Captain on deck.' And I'm still not sure if he was referring to me or him, but it was beautiful either way. The other reason I loved it so much was, well, obviously, the performances. We put two cameras on Summer and Sean so they could do the scene together and not in faked coverage, and Jack lit it so simply — a little light above, a little light below — it was just in a tiny space, there were no camera moves to speak of, just two actors lit incomparably beautifully and doing their thing extraordinarily well. And the places Summer goes to and the way Sean stays with her and supports her in that scene I find just heartrending. A lot of things came together. That was a good day. And then any day when we blew shit up.

What is the main difference in having months of post-production on a feature vs. weeks of post-production in TV?

It absolutely has been useful, because it's given me time, not just to look at [Serenity] with [test screening] audiences who have never seen the show and go, 'Now, what do I really need to tell them, what is the strongest way to get each scene across?', but it's given me the time to step back in what is often a very frantic process as a filmmaker. Having gone through a lot of editing and cutting and tests and changes, putting scenes in, taking them out, putting them back — you lose the woods for the trees. And the extra time has given me time to look at the woods again and say, 'Okay, what have I intended with this film, what have I accomplished, and is there anything that is missing, both in how I'm reaching the audience and in what I'm telling them?' And it's been terrific. Plus the people we have brought on, making changes, they've done stellar work and I feel the film will be absolutely elevated by the fact that it had just a little more time to make.

What has the fan reaction been like in the run up to the release?

The first [test] screening was not very carefully screened [to make sure audience members were impartial], and so the fans showed up and the executives literally came out saying, 'We've never had an experience like that. I mean, we understand that these test results might be somewhat skewed, but oh, my God.' They were sweating. They were high. It was quite an extraordinary thing. And the fans — manning booths for *Serenity*, paid for by themselves. The incredible amount of [fan] support and the intensity of it has always informed not just the studio's enthusiasm, but their strategies and how they want to handle marketing and they're very respectful of what the fans bring to the party and they're very anxious to make sure that the fans don't get lost in the very legitimate effort to bring this movie to people who've never heard of the show.

Where is the *Serenity* universe going from here?

There are three issues of a comic book that will be compiled into a graphic novel, or novella. It is kind of a bridge, really, between the show and the movie. In the show, Inara swore she would leave; in the movie, she has left and so has Book and the comic book is about an adventure that deals with both of those things and also an old enemy of theirs from the show and all sorts of fun. Beyond the film, where *Serenity* is going is anybody's guess. If the film doesn't make any money at all, my guess is that *Serenity* is going back into my heart. If the film does well, there could be more movies.

Has the experience of making *Serenity* been what you had hoped/expected it to be?

It's much better and much harder than I thought it was going to be.

Better, because I managed to find people — and luck had a lot to do with it — for my film crew who were as much a family as my TV crew was. I landed the incomparable Jack Green as my d.p. [director of photography] and he runs an incredibly efficient and amiable set. I would have settled for either. I am in awe of him. The people he chooses to have around him — three of whom coincidentally bore the last name Green, because it was very much a family affair — really had a lot to do with what it feels like to make the movie. Rich Sickler, my a.d. [assistant director], also brought a lot of that — a lot of efficiency, and always with sweetness. And between the two of them, they made sure that we got a hundred days of filming done in sixty days, that we could make an eighty-million-dollar movie for substantially less than that. They really gave me so much. And of course, being back with my dear friends who play this crew [of the ship Serenity in] an atmosphere where the studio was completely behind us and incredibly supportive. [The actors] were so blown away by that, because the last time we were together, we were constantly under threat of cancellation. And here we were, where we had a much bigger, riskier project, and all we got from the executives upstairs was good vibes and support and help when we needed it, and that was really great.

Harder, because I've been an executive producer for eight years, which is like being a teacher. You're basically teaching people how to write your show and how to make your show and how to act it and how to direct it and everything else. And then I found myself in the position of student. I found myself learning, and by learning, I do mean making mistakes, really starting from Square One in a lot of ways. And that was very humbling and very difficult, and sometimes very frustrating, but ultimately the best thing in the world. Mary Parent, the executive who championed the project from the start and oversaw it, has taught me more about making movies than anybody in my life since [Jeanine Basinger] my professor at school.

This is my first movie and I just hope people will keep that in mind [laughs]. It's very, very personal, it's very, very political, it's very, very emotional and hopefully nobody will notice any of those things, because they'll be too busy having fun. That's my mandate for everything I do. ■

Joss Whedon was interviewed by Abbie Bernstein.

NIL MADOC REES '04

THE SHOOTING SCRIPT

EXT. SPACE - VFX

We see the Earth.

White pops blossom on the surface, and moments later ships — huge, intricate space-freighters — come roaring from the surface, passing camera with a thunder of gas and flame.

We hear a woman's voice:

VOICE OVER
Earth-That-Was could no longer sustain our numbers, we were so many.

We see a solar system; a sun like our own, surrounded by many more planets than ours, they in turn surrounded by moons.

VOICE OVER
We found a new solar system: dozens of planets and hundreds of moons.

We see a terraform station; a bunker-like complex many miles across, air billowing from it, electricity running over it.

VOICE OVER
Each one terraformed — a process taking decades — to support human life. To be new Earths.

We see a futuristic megalopolis, gleaming and cool.

VOICE OVER
The Central Planets were the first settled and are the most advanced, embodying civilization at its peak.

We see an empty desert plain, then pull out to see the entire planet — and further, to see we're on the edge of the galaxy.

VOICE OVER
Life on the outer planets is much more primitive, and difficult. That's why the Central planets formed the Alliance, so everyone can enjoy the comfort and enlightenment of true civiliza-tion. That's why we fought the War for Unification.

During this a woman steps in front of the last image and we see it is on a wall screen in a:

EXT. CLASSROOM - DAY

It's a group of twelve-year-olds, serious and well dressed. They sit on their heels under a sparsely elegant tent, small wooden desks with embedded screens in front of them. The tent is on a lawn surrounded by lush foliage. People walk about and vehicles glide quietly overhead. A utopian vista.

GIRL #1
Now that the war's over, our soldiers get to come home, yes?

TEACHER
Some of them. Some will be sta-tioned on the rim planets as Peace Enforcers.

BOY #1
I don't understand. Why were the Independents even fighting us? Why wouldn't they look to be more civilized?

Left: The young River Tam (Hunter Ansley Wryn).

Below: Design concept for River's school desk.

TEACHER
That's a good question. Does anybody want to open on that?

GIRL #2
I hear they're cannibals.

BOY #2
That's only Reavers.

GIRL #3
Reavers aren't real.

BOY #2
Full well they are. They attack settlers from space, they kill them and wear their skins and rape them for hours and hours —

TEACHER
(Chinese)
BAI-tuo, AN-jing-eedyen!
[English: We will enjoy your silence now!]
(continued; calmer)
It's true that there are... dangers on the outer planets. So let's follow up on Borodin's question. With all the social and medical advancements we can bring to the independents, why would they fight so hard against us?

RIVER
We meddle.

TEACHER
River?
(Chinese)
Shuh-MUH?
[English: I'm sorry?]

RIVER is a dark, intense little girl, writing with one hand and "typing" with the other. (Typing consists of holding a long wooden stylus and tapping either end down different columns of chinese characters on her desktop screen.) She is a good two years younger than the other kids.

RIVER
People don't like to be meddled

with. We tell them what to do, what to think, don't run don't walk we're in their homes and in their heads and we haven't the right. We're meddlesome.

TEACHER
(gently taking her stylus)
River, we're not telling people what to think. We're just trying to show them how.

She violently PLUNGES the stylus into the girl's forehead —

INT. LAB - DAY

And we FLASH CUT to the actual present: a 16 year old RIVER sitting in a metal chair, needles stuck in her skull (one right where the teacher had stuck her) being adjusted by a technician. A second monitors her brain patterns.

The lab is cold, blue, steel. Insidiously clean.

2ND TECHNICIAN
She's dreaming.

Opposite page: Two designs for Simon's baton.

Below: River in Doctor Mathias' lab.

FIRST TECHNICIAN
Nightmare?

2ND TECHNICIAN
Off the charts. Scary monsters.

DOCTOR MATHIAS
Let's amp it up. Delcium, eight-drop.

DOCTOR MATHIAS is not instantly likable — nor gradually, for that matter. A cold man, and more than a little satisfied with himself. He carries a clipboard as he addresses the GOVERNMENT INSPECTOR, observing.
And making him a little nervous.

The Inspector is in shadow, but his uniform indicates substantial rank, as does the eagle-crested baton — no longer than a ruler — that he clutches in one gloved hand.

DOCTOR MATHIAS
See, most of our best work is done when they're asleep. We can monitor and direct their subconscious, implant suggestions...

River starts convulsing, mewing in misery. The Inspector starts forward, slowly.

DOCTOR MATHIAS
It's a little startling to see, but the results are spectacular. Especially in this case. River Tam is our star pupil.

The Inspector steps into the light. He is rigid, cold, staring at the girl with no emotion at all. His name, as we will very soon learn, is SIMON.

SIMON
I've heard that.

DOCTOR MATHIAS
She's a genius. Her mental capacity is extraordinary, even with the side-effects.

SIMON
Tell me about them.

DOCTOR MATHIAS
Well, obviously, she's unstable... the neural stripping gives them

heightened cognitive reception, but it also destabilizes their own reality matrix. It manifests as borderline schizophrenia... which at this point is the price for being truly psychic.

SIMON
(moves toward her)
What use do we have for a psychic if she's insane?

DOCTOR MATHIAS
I don't have to tell you the security potential of someone who can read minds. And she has lucid periods — we hope to improve upon the... I'm sorry, Sir, I have to ask if there's some reason for this inspection.

SIMON
(turning)
Am I making you nervous?

DOCTOR MATHIAS
Key members of Parliament have personally observed this subject. I was told their support for the project was unanimous. The demonstration of her power —

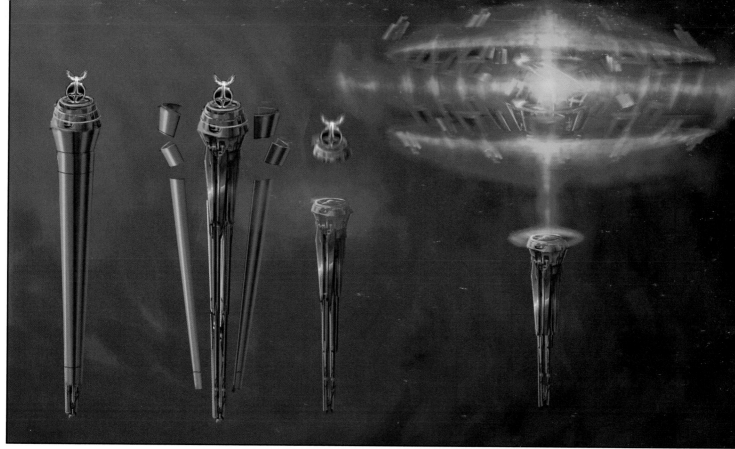

SIMON
(turns back to her)
How is she physically?

DOCTOR MATHIAS
Like nothing we've seen. All our subjects are conditioned for combat, but River... she's a creature of extraordinary grace.

SIMON
Yes. She always did love to dance.

He drops to one knee, slamming his baton to the floor.

ANGLE: THE BATON

As the top pops off like a bouncing betty (the grenade), flying up over Simon and River's heads and then bursting forth in a flat circle of blue energy that bisects the room, flowing through the staff's heads and knocking them out.

Simon rushes to River, gently removes the probes from her head and swabs her, whispering:

SIMON
River. Wake up. Please, it's Simon. River. It's your brother. Wake up...

She begins to stir as a noise moves him to the door, looking out and removing his uniform to reveal an orderly's tunic beneath.

River is suddenly next to him. He jumps a little.

RIVER
Simon.

A beat, as they face each other, Simon fighting emotion.

RIVER
They know you've come.

INT. GUARD STATION - CONTINUING

As a guard looks at a monitor. He mostly resembles a secret service man — more bureaucrat than thug. A second man rolls into frame on a chair behind him, also watching the screen.

INT. RESEARCH CENTER CORRIDOR - CONTINUING

Simon walks River through the corridor. They approach a pair of double doors.

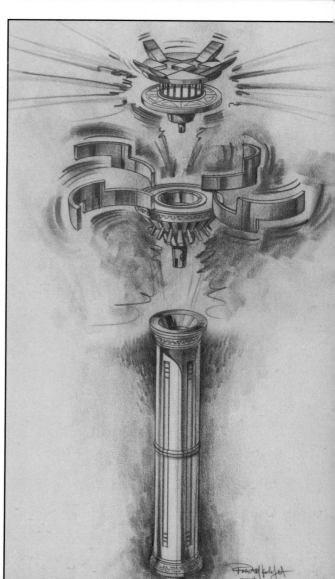

SIMON
We can't make it to the surface from inside.

Simon turns suddenly as he hears footsteps, people heading at them from the other side of the doors.

SIMON
Find a —

But River has, impossibly, scampered up over some lab equipment to the dark top of the corridor, where she holds herself in a perfect split, feet against the walls and outstretched hand holding the sprinkler for support.

The doors burst open and two doctors pass by, hardly noticing the lone orderly. Passing right under River.

EXT. VENTILATION SHAFT - MOMENTS LATER

It's small, 15 feet by 15 feet. Goes a long way up and a long way down. One wide hinged window looks in on the hall inside. Simon and River approach with quiet haste.

They slip through the window. Simon shuts it, wedges his baton into the handle as the SECURITY AGENTS APPROACH. They fire at the glass, but their lasers have no effect.

Wind whips River's hair about as she looks up to see a small patch of daylight visible ten stories up. Sees the sky blotted out by a small ship that hovers above them.

EXT. ABOVE LAB FACILITY - VFX

THE SHIP is floating over the grass of rolling hills, the city gleaming far beyond. This facility is well hidden.

WIL MADOC REES '04 'SERENITY'

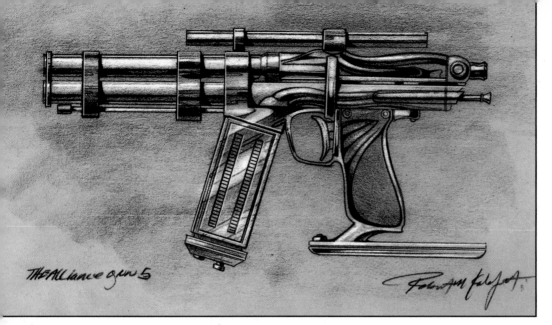

THE ALLIANCE GUN 5

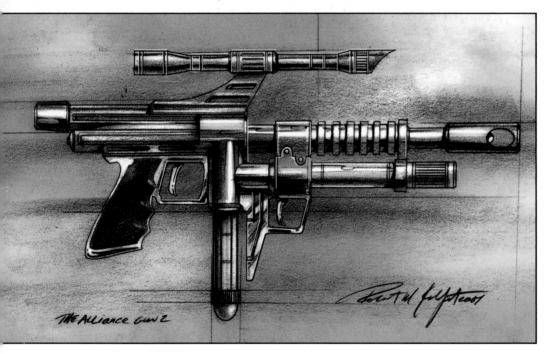

THE ALLIANCE GUN 2

Above: Designs for weaponry carried by the Alliance Security Agents.

EXT. VENTILATION SHAFT - DAY

A gurney-sized section of the ship's belly detaches and drops down ten stories, cables spooling it out of the ship. It comes to Simon and River and stops suddenly.

SIMON
Get on!

He is standing by the window — and the Security Agent is right behind him, PUNCHING the window with all his might.

Simon helps River onto the gurney, then jumps on himself as the

Security Agent cracks the glass. The two are whisked up in the gurney, River on her knees, Simon standing beside her holding one of the cables —

THE OPERATIVE (O.S.)
Stop.

The action freezes.

THE OPERATIVE (O.S.)
Lovely. Lovely. Backtrack.

The action REVERSES, taking us back to the moment of Simon and River on the gurney just before it rises.

THE OPERATIVE (O.S.)
Stop.

There is a motionless beat, River frozen in that crouch, and he steps through what we now see is a hologram of the event. The Government's man. We'll just call him THE OPERATIVE.

He is thoughtful, a little removed. Wire-rimmed glasses, a suit too nondescript to be a uniform, too neat to be casual wear. He is in:

INT. INSTITUTE RECORDS ROOM - DAY

— which is long and bare but for drawers of holographic records, a set-up for watching recordings (where the image of Simon and River floats), and a table with computer and chair. The Operative crosses to the table, looks over some papers.

THE OPERATIVE
Biograph. Simon Tam.

CLOSE ON: THE OPERATIVE'S GLASSES

As Simon's history files down in print and pictures — graduation, security photo from his medical internship — over one lens of the Operative's glasses.

THE OPERATIVE
Remarkable children.

Doctor Mathias storms in, two security men (not the ones from the opening) and a nervous young female intern following. Mathias looks greyer and more gaunt than when we saw him last.

DOCTOR MATHIAS
Excuse me! No one is allowed in the records room without my express permission.

THE OPERATIVE
(over this, quietly)
Enter the doctor.
(to Mathias)
Forgive me. I prefer to see the event alone, without bias.

Mathias looks at the hologram — realizes which one it is.

DOCTOR MATHIAS
I need to see your clearance.

THE OPERATIVE
You're right to insist. I know you've had security issues here.

He places his hand on a screen as he says it. Mathias looks at the readout, and drops the bluster.

DOCTOR MATHIAS
Apologies. An Operative of the Parliament will of course have full cooperation.
(looks at screen)

I'm not sure what... I see no listing of rank, or name.

THE OPERATIVE
I have neither. Like this facility, I don't exist. The Parliament calls me in when...
when they wish they didn't have to. Let's talk about the Tams.

DOCTOR MATHIAS
I assume you've scanned the status logs...

THE OPERATIVE
River was your greatest success. A prodigy — A phenomenon. Until her brother walked in eight months ago and took her from you.

DOCTOR MATHIAS
It's not quite so simple.

THE OPERATIVE
I'm very aware of that.

DOCTOR MATHIAS
He came in with full creds. He beat the ap-scan, the retinal... There was no way I could —

THE OPERATIVE
No, no. Of course. The boy spent his fortune developing the contacts to infiltrate this place.

DOCTOR MATHIAS
Gave up a brilliant future in medicine as well, you've probably read. Turned his back on his whole life. Madness.

THE OPERATIVE
Madness, no. Something a good deal more dangerous. Have you looked at this scan carefully? At his face?

Mathias looks uncertain.

THE OPERATIVE
It's love, in point of fact. He loved his sister and he knew she was in pain. So he took her somewhere safe.

Above: The hologram of River, frozen in mid-escape.

SUMMER GLAU

What makes this film so special is the amazing character development. There's heists, there's Reavers freaking out, there's the Mal and Inara relationship going strong — lots of controversy. Every character has their big hero moment, something that's really, really cool that they get to do. I get more than few of my own special moments, that have been unbelievably fun. River's around more than she was in the series. She's starting to recover. There's a lot more to her character. In the series there were so many things that weren't explained or divulged, but now people are going to learn so much more about River. There's a lot of action too. I'm not the timid wilting flower in the corner forever...

DOCTOR MATHIAS
Why are you here?

THE OPERATIVE
I'm here because the situation is
even less simple than you think.
(eyeing him)
Do you know what your sin is,
Doctor?

DOCTOR MATHIAS
I... I would be very careful about
what you —

THE OPERATIVE
(sadly)
It's pride.

He touches a small control stand
near the hologram and the holo-
gramic image jumps to the Doctor
and Simon in the lab, Mathias
repeating:

DOCTOR MATHIAS
Key members of Parliament have
personally observed this subject. I
was told their support —

THE OPERATIVE
(shutting it off)
Key members of Parliament. Key.
The minds behind every diplomat-
ic, military and covert operation in
the galaxy, and you put them in a
room with a psychic.

DOCTOR MATHIAS
She was... she read cards, nothing
more.

THE OPERATIVE
It's come to our attention that
River became much more unstable, more... disturbed, after you
showed her off to Parliament. Did
she see something very terrible in
those cards?

DOCTOR MATHIAS
If there was some... classified information that she... well she never
spoke of it.
(hurriedly)
I don't know what it is.

THE OPERATIVE
Nor do I. And judging by her dete-
riorating mental state I'd say we're
both better off. Secrets are not my
concern. Keeping them is.

DOCTOR MATHIAS
Whatever... secrets she might have
accidentally gleaned... it's probable
she doesn't even know she knows
them. That they're buried beneath
layers of psychosis —

THE OPERATIVE
But they are in her. Her mind is
unquiet.
It's the will of the Parliament that I

kill her. And the brother. Because
of your sin.
(moving to his briefcase)
You know, in certain older civilized
cultures, when men failed as
entirely as you have, they would
throw themselves on their
swords.

DOCTOR MATHIAS
(fed up)
Well, unfortunately I forgot to
bring a sword to —

The air rings crisply as the
Operative pulls out his sword.

THE OPERATIVE
The Parliament has no further
interest in psychics. They represent a threat to the harmony and
stability of our Alliance.

DOCTOR MATHIAS
I would put that down right now if I
were you.

THE OPERATIVE
Would you be killed in your sleep,
like an ailing pet? Whatever your
failings, I believe you deserve better
than that.

The agents move. He slices the
throat of the one behind him with
true grace, thrusting at the second

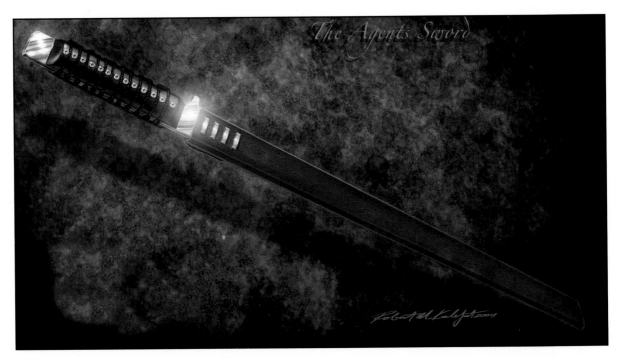

as he's pulling out his gun and pinning his hand. A moment, and the dying agent reflexively squeezes the trigger, shooting his own arm.

The Operative pulls out the sword and the agent falls as quietly as the first.

Mathias bolts but the Operative pins him to the wall. He bunches his fingers and jabs the side of the Doctor's spine. Mathias stiffens, suddenly, agonizingly immobile.

The Operative steps back, observes the Doctor's rigid grimace for a moment. Almost ceremoniously, he drops to one knee and holds the blade out to one side, hilt to the floor and point tilted toward the doctor. The Doctor stares at it in horror as his paralyzed body begins to tip over toward it.
The Operative turns toward the terrified intern at the door.

THE OPERATIVE
Young miss, I'll need all the logs on behavioral modification triggers. We'll have to reach out to River Tam, and help her to come back to us. No matter how far out Simon has taken her, we can —

He's almost startled when the Doctor's body drops into frame, slowed suddenly by the sword. It squeaks down the blade, the Doctor unable to cry out, as the Operative whispers to him:

THE OPERATIVE
This is a good death. There's no shame in this, in a man's death. A man who's done fine works. We're making a better world. All of them, better worlds.

Mathias is dead. The Operative pulls the sword out as the body rolls over. As he wipes the sword down:

THE OPERATIVE
Young miss, I need you to get to

work now. I think I may have a long way to travel.

She goes. He approaches River, very close, staring...

THE OPERATIVE
Where are you hiding, little girl?

The noise is sucked suddenly out of the room as we black out.

SERENITY

... becomes the name painted on the side of a spaceship, with the same in Chinese behind it.

EXT. SPACE, ORBITING THE MOON "LILAC" - DAY

We move away from the ship. The name is on the nose, under the bridge. It sticks out from the body of the ship like a craning neck. The body is bulbous, with propulsion engines on either side and a giant glowing back.

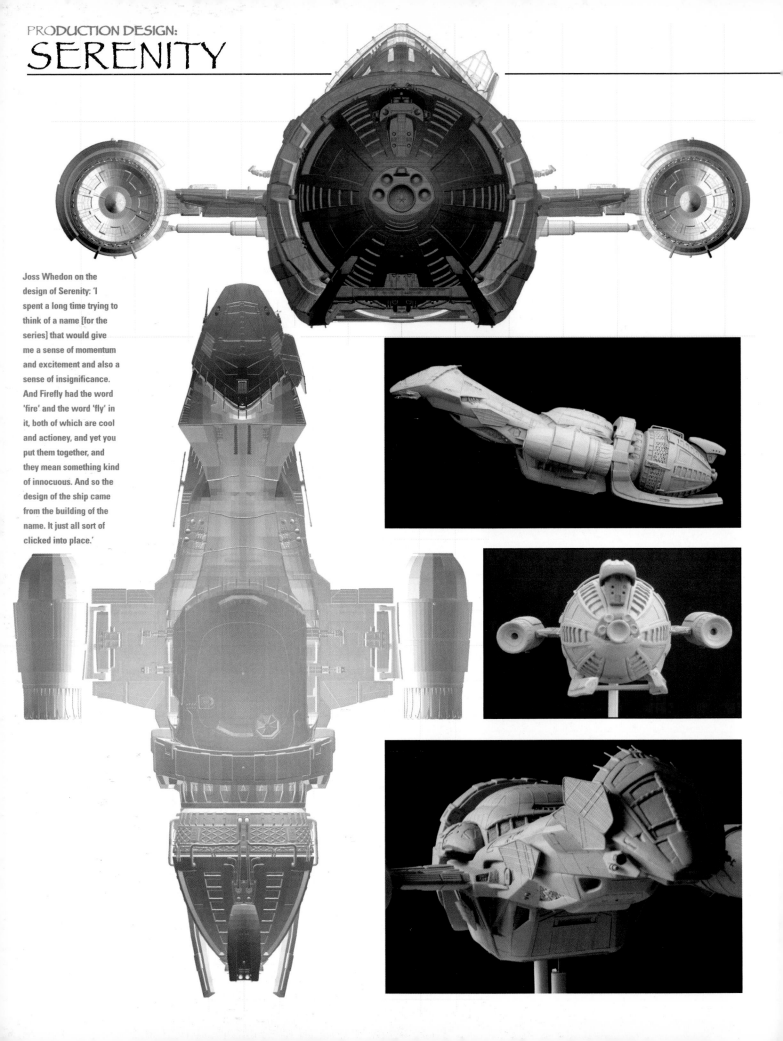

Joss Whedon on the design of Serenity: 'I spent a long time trying to think of a name [for the series] that would give me a sense of momentum and excitement and also a sense of insignificance. And Firefly had the word 'fire' and the word 'fly' in it, both of which are cool and actioney, and yet you put them together, and they mean something kind of innocuous. And so the design of the ship came from the building of the name. It just all sort of clicked into place.'

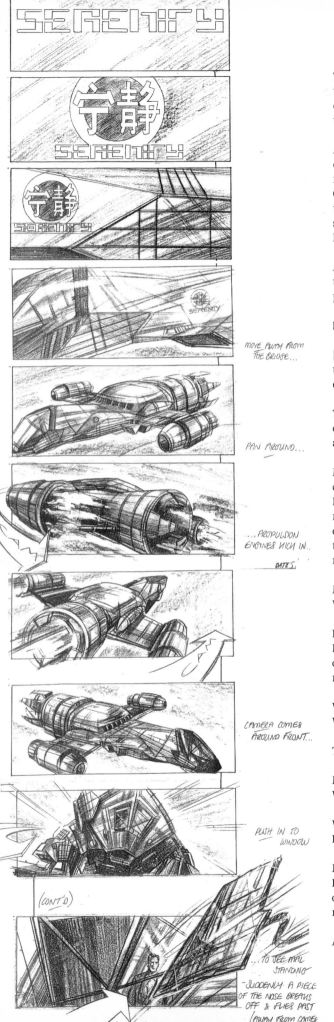

There are two small shuttles tucked in over the 'wings' of the engines. It's not the sleekest ship in the 'verse, to be sure.

As it hits atmo, the propulsion engines take over and she starts to rock a bit, noise filling our ears. Camera comes around the front, at the windows and into the bridge, to see the Captain, MALCOLM 'MAL' REYNOLDS, standing and watching.

At that moment, a small piece of the nose breaks off and goes flying past the window.

INT. BRIDGE - CONTINUING

[Note: the following sequence will take us through the ship in one extended STEADICAM shot.]

The bridge is small: two pilot seats on either side, and a tangle of wires and machinery all about.

Mal wears the knee-length brown coat and boots of an old Independent. Gun at his hip. He's not unlike the ship — he's seen a bit of the world and it left him, emotionally at least, weathered. Right now, though, he's mostly startled.

MAL
What was that?

He's addressing the pilot, WASH. Flight gear and a hawaiian shirt, toy dinosaurs populating his station — no old soldier, but just as startled.

WASH
Whoa! Did you see that —

The ship bucks —

MAL
Was that the primary buffer panel?

WASH
It did seem to resemble –

MAL
Did the Primary Buffer Panel just fall off my gorramn ship for no apparent reason?

Another buck —

WASH
Looks like.

MAL
I thought Kaylee checked our entry couplings! I have a very clear memory of it —

WASH
Yeah well if she doesn't give us some extra flow from the engine room to offset the burnthrough this landing is gonna get pretty interesting.

MAL
Define "Interesting".

WASH
(calm suggestion:)
"Oh god, oh god, we're all gonna die?"

MAL
(hits the com)
This is the Captain. There's a little problem with our entry sequence; we may experience slight turbulence and then explode.
(to Wash, exiting)
Can you shave the vector —

WASH
I'm doing it! It's not enough.
(hits com)
Kaylee!

MAL
Just get us on the ground!

WASH
That part'll happen, pretty definitely.

INT. FOREDECK HALL - CONTINUING

The camera leads Mal down. On either side of the hall are ladders leading down to crew's personal quarters.

The hulking mercenary JAYNE is coming up out of his bunk as Mal passes. He carries a number of rifles and grenades.

JAYNE
We're gonna explode? I don't wanna explode.

Jane Rifle

MAL
Jayne, how many weapons you plan on bringing? You only got the two arms...

JAYNE
I just get excitable as to choice, like to have my options open.

MAL
I don't plan on any shooting taking place during this job.

JAYNE
Well, what you plan and what takes place ain't ever exactly been similar.

MAL
No grenades.
(Jayne groans)
No grenades.

First Mate ZOE enters from the lower level. Her mode of dress and military deference mark her as a war buddy of Mal's.

ZOE
Are we crashing again?

MAL
Talk to your husband. Is the Mule prepped?

ZOE
Good to go, sir. Just loading her up.
(to Jayne)
Are those grenades?

JAYNE
Cap'n doesn't want 'em.

ZOE
We're robbing the place. We're not occupying it.

All that plays in the background as we lead Mal into the:

INT. DINING ROOM - CONTINUING

It's the communal space of the ship, homey and messy. There is food left lying on the table. Mal swipes a dumpling from a plate, pops it in his mouth as another jolt rocks him and sends most of the tableware clattering to the floor.

MAL
(calling out)
Kaylee!

He enters:

INT. AFT HALL/ENGINE ROOM - CONTINUING

MAL
(still calling)
Kaylee, what in the sphincter of hell are you playing at?

The hall leads to the rust-brown chaos that is the engine room. Working around the engine in a forest of wires, sparks and smoke is the sweetly pretty mechanic, KAYLEE. She passes Mal with a slightly impatient smile as he stands in the doorway, raising his voice above the din.

MAL
We got the Primary Buffer —

KAYLEE
Everything's shiny, Cap'n. Not to fret.

MAL
You told me —
(jolt)
You told me the entry couplings would hold for another week!

KAYLEE
(working)
That was six months ago, cap'n.

Opposite: Storyboard for the beginning of the extended shot that introduces Serenity and her crew.

Above: Concept design for one of Jayne's many, many weapons.

MAL
My ship don't crash. If she crashes, you crashed her.

Steam and electricity shoot at him, backing him up.

He turns to see Simon behind him. Simon is more seasoned than before, but still contrasts the Captain entirely in dress and manner. He is implacably proper. Also pissed.

MAL
Doctor. Guess I need to get innocked 'fore we hit planetside.

Simon nods, the ship jolting again.

SEAN MAHER

Serenity is sort of a renegade ship. Captain Reynolds, Zoe, all the characters on the ship, teeter on the edge of space, making their way, finding work, job to job. Usually not the most legal of activities. My character Simon is, in high contrast to them, from a very privileged background. He's a doctor, and he has a sister, who was a prodigy when she was growing up. So, our family sent her away, to what we thought was a government-sponsored academic program that would further her learning. But then I found out that the government has been running these horrible tests on her, screwing with her brain, so I risk everything to get her out. And we end up on Serenity, as fugitives running from the government. I'm constantly trying to figure out what exactly has been done to my sister, what the tests were about, and what's wrong with her. I dedicate my time, and energy, to figuring that out and helping her.

MAL
Bit of a rockety ride. Nothing to worry about.

SIMON
I'm not worried.

MAL
Fear is nothing to be ashamed of, Doc.

SIMON
This isn't fear. This is anger.

MAL
(laughs)
Well, it's kinda hard to tell the one from t'other, face like yours.

SIMON
I imagine if it were fear, my eyes would be wider.

MAL
I'll look for that next time.

SIMON
You're not taking her.

MAL
(brushing past him)
No no, that's not a thing I'm interested in talking over with —

SIMON
She's not going with you. That's final.

MAL
(turning back)

I hear the words "that's final" come out of your mouth ever again, they truly will be.
(turning away again)
This is my boat. Y'all are guests on it.

He heads down a side corridor that has steps leading down to:

INT. PASSENGER DORM - CONTINUING

Simon is right on his heels as we lead them down the stairs.

SIMON
Guests? I earn my passage, Captain —

MAL
And it's time your little sister learned from your fine example.

SIMON
I've earned my passage treating bullet holes, knife wounds, laser burns...

MAL
Some of our jobs are trickier than others —

SIMON
And you want to put my sister in the middle of that.

MAL
Didn't say 'want'. Said 'will'. It's one job, Doc. She'll be fine.

The passenger dorm has a time-worn warmth that most of the ship shares. Except, of course, for the sterile blue of:

INT. INFIRMARY - CONTINUING

Into which the two men step.

SIMON
She's a seventeen year old girl. A mentally traumatized sevente—

MAL
She's a reader. Sees into the truth of things; might see trouble before it's coming. Which is of use to me.

SIMON
And that's your guiding star, isn't it? What's of use.

MAL
(laughs)
Honestly, doctor, I think we may really crash this time anyway.

Simon jabs the inoculation needle into Mal's arm.

SIMON
Do you understand what I've gone through to keep River away from the Alliance?

MAL
I do, and it's a fact we here have been courteous enough to keep to our own selves.

SIMON
Are you threatening to —

MAL
I look out for me and mine. That don't include you less I conjure it does. Now you stuck a thorn in the Alliance's paw and that tickles me a bit. But it also means I gotta step twice as fast to avoid them, and that means turning down plenty of jobs. Even honest ones.

He starts away, Simon still keeping pace.

MAL
Every year since the war the Alliance pushes further out, fences off another piece of the 'verse. Come a day there won't be room for naughty men like us to slip about at all. This job goes south, there well may not be another.

INT. CARGO BAY - CONTINUING

They enter the biggest space on the ship. Giant doors sit at the front, which will open upon landing to reveal a lowering ramp. Catwalks surround the space, leading up at the front to the foredeck hall. We've come all the way through Serenity.

MAL
So here is us, on the raggedy edge.

Opposite: A behind-the-scenes shot of Serenity's cargo bay.

Below: A behind-the-scenes shot of Serenity's hovercraft, the Mule. The cables were digitally removed in post-production.

The look of Serenity's four-man hovercraft went through several approaches before it was narrowed down to a final version. A full sized vehicle was then built for filming.

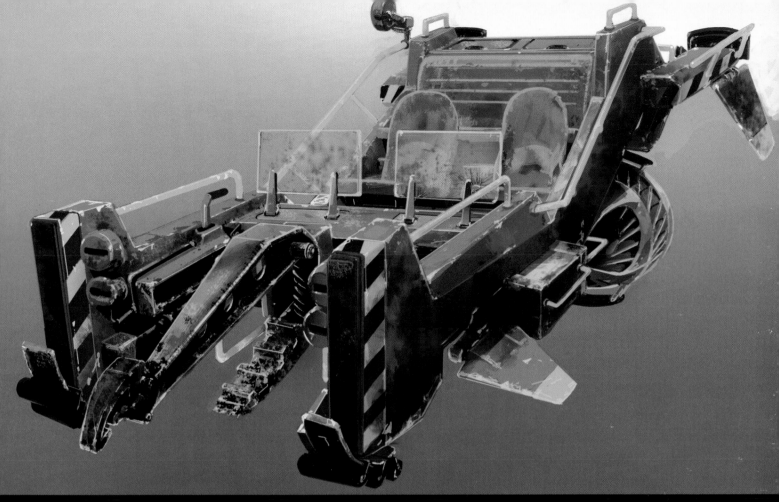

Don't push me and I won't push you.
(Chinese)
DONG-luh-MAH?
[English: Are we clear here?]

Simon starts up the stairs. As Mal walks on, we tilt up to see the Mule, a four-man hovercraft hanging from chains near the ceiling. Jayne and Zoe are tossing duffle bags into it.

MAL
Zoe, is Wash gonna straighten this boat out before we get flattened?

ZOE
Like a downy feather, sir. Nobody flies like my mister.

The camera picks up Simon's feet as they enter foreground on the catwalk, and track with them to find:

SIMON
River...

She's lying on her side, looking straight at us. A loose summer dress draped over her small frame.

RIVER
I know. We're going for a ride.

EXT. LILAC - DESERT GULCH - DAY

Serenity settles gently down as the cargo bay door opens.

INT. CARGO BAY - CONTINUING

The chains are hoisted back up into the ceiling of the ship. The Mule floats just above the floor, Jayne throwing extra clips in the container next to River in the back. Simon is handing River her boots, which she hands back.

SIMON
Now, River, you stay behind the others. If there's fighting you drop to the floor or run away. It's okay to leave them to die.

River puts on a huge pair of goggles, looks at her brother.

RIVER
I'm the brains of the operation.

ZOE
We should hit town right during Sunday worship. Won't be any crowds.

MAL
If Fanty and Mingo are right about the payroll, this could look to be a sunny day for us.

SIMON
(approaching)
Captain, I'll ask you one last time...

MAL
Doctor, I'm taking your sister under my protection here. If anything happens to her, anything at all, I swear to you I will get very choked up. Honestly. There could be tears.

He peels out, leaves Simon fuming — and realizing he's still holding River's boots... Kaylee sidles up to him...

KAYLEE
Don't mind the Captain none, Simon. I know he'll look out for her.

SIMON
It's amazing. I bring River all the way out to the raggedy edge of the 'verse so she can hide from the Alliance by robbing banks.

KAYLEE
It's just a little Trading Station. They'll be back 'fore you can spit.
(as he stalks off)
Not that you spit...

Kaylee watches him go, a tad forlorn.

EXT. LILAC - DAY

We see the town sprawled before us, as the Mule heads in.

The town embodies the lives of folk out here: adobe and wood mix with metal and plastic — whatever's on hand to build with. Right now the streets are mainly empty.

EXT. TRADING STATION - CONTINUING

The Mule pulls up, Zoe hitching it as they speak:

JAYNE
What are we hoping to find here that equals the worth of a turd?

MAL
Security payroll. Alliance don't have the manpower to "enforce the peace" on every border moon cluster— they hire out to the private firms, who will not work for credit. They get paid in cashy money, which once a month rests here.

JAYNE
Don't that lead back to the Alliance anyhow?

ZOE
No private firm would ever report a theft of its own payroll. They'd appear weak, might lose their contract.

MAL
We're as ghosts in this. Won't but rattle the floor.

JAYNE
(cocks his gun)

Shiny. Let's be bad guys.

Mal turns back to River.

MAL
You ready to go to work, darlin'?

RIVER
There's no pattern to the pebbles here, they're completely random. I tried to count them but you drove too fast. Hummingbird.

MAL
(never mind)
Right. Great. Let's go.

INT. TRADING STATION - DAY

We are in a camera's eye view, right above the door.

The door slams open, Mal and Jayne stride in, Zoe following and whipping her hogleg right at camera without looking. Reverse to see the camera is also a small screen with "Welcome to Lilac" on it for the millisecond before it's blown to bits.

There's maybe fifteen people in the place: store workers, farm-folk

Top: Concept art of a Lilac town building.

Above: Zoe and Jayne, ready to be bad guys.

Below: Concept designs for Mal's gun. Joss Whedon: 'I was looking for hardware. I was looking for clunky, old-fashioned. I had Mal's gun designed very specifically after a Civil War-era pistol à la *The Outlaw Josey Wales*. It had those lines exactly, which are rounder and longer than most guns that we think of, yet at the same time, in a casing that gave it a completely futuristic outer shape.'

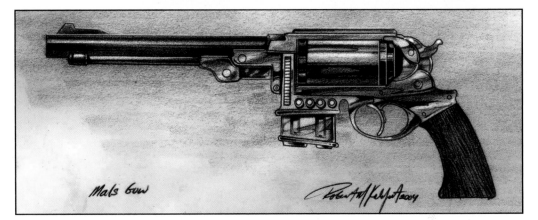

Mal's Gun

and a couple dirt-poor kids. It's a combination post-office, general store, bank, and most other things.

MAL
Hands and knees and heads bowed down! Everybody, now!

Two men who appear to be farm folk rush Mal and the others. Mal draws on the elder one and he stops dead in his tracks. Mal's gun is long, not unlike Civil War era issue, but very much new in design.

The other tries to tackle Jayne, which is not necessarily a great idea. Jayne clotheslines him so hard he spins right upside-down — and Jayne grabs him by the legs and CRACK! — bounces his head right off the floor, knocking him out cold.

MAL
Y'all wanna be looking very intently at your own belly buttons. I see a head start to rise, violence is gonna ensue.

The guy who rushed Mal complies along with everyone else. Jayne dumps his catch on the floor and rips open his dirty shirt to reveal a private security uniform.

JAYNE
Looks like this is the place.

He takes a shiny official pin from the guard he's clocked and looks up at Mal, who motions for Zoe to open the front door. She does, and River steps in.

ANGLE: RIVER'S BARE FEET — walking slowly among the hunched-over customers as Mal addresses them.

MAL
You've probably guessed we mean to be thieving here, but what we are after is not yours. So let's have no undue fussing.

As he is speaking, Jayne scrambles to the back office, finding the small vault locked.

JAYNE
She's locked up.

River suddenly looks around, perturbed.

CLOSE ON: a YOUNG TOUGH.

River looks up at Zoe, alarmed, and silently points to the young man. He is slowly reaching for the weapon in his belt.

He finds Zoe's sawed-off nuzzling his cheek.

ZOE
You know what the definition of a hero is? It's someone who gets other people killed. You can look it up later.

He drops his weapon, slides it across the floor.

Mal moves to the Trade Agent. Hauls him up, tosses him toward the vault. Zoe and Jayne follow.

TRADE AGENT
This is just a crop moon, don't think you'll find what you —

MAL
(Chinese)
BEE-tzway. Wrong wuomun FAH-TSAI.
[English: Shut up and make us wealthy.]

The old man punches in the code.

Above: Production design art of the Trading Station, 'a combination post-office, general store, bank, and most other things.'

What opens is a tiny wall safe.
Bundles of bills, some scattered
coin. Unimpressive. Jayne and
Zoe are behind the captain,
peering in.

ZOE
At last. We can retire and give up
this life of crime.

Mal reaches in, pulls a lever and
the floor opens, a six foot hole
appearing, stairs leading to a corridor, all gleaming metal and blue
light. Zoe smiles. Jayne peers
down as Mal addresses the Trade
Agent.

MAL
(to the Trade Agent)
Is there a guard down there? Be
truthful.

TRADE AGENT
(nodding)
Y'all are Browncoats, hey? Fought
for independence?

MAL
War's long done. We're all just
folk now.
(calls down)
Listen up! We are coming down to
empty that vault!

The voice of a young GUARD
comes up from below.

GUARD (O.S.)
You have to give me your authori-
zation password!

Jayne impatiently fires a burst of
machine-gun fire down into the
hole. A beat...

GUARD (O.S.)
Okay...

Mal looks at Zoe and they head
down into:

INT. VAULT - CONTINUING

Which is as modern as something
off the Central Planets. A short
corridor leads to a real vault door,
that the guard is already opening.
Behind that door, a few bags of
the real deal: neatly stacked cash,
waiting to be robbed.

**INT. TRADING STATION -
CONTINUING**

We move in on River as something crosses her face. Worry.

EXT. TOWN - DAY

A WOMAN carrying a bucket and
her nine year old SON are looking
at the trading station a few buildings away.

SON
Repeater.

WOMAN
Did sound summat like gun-
blast... Maybe you aught run
tell Lawman...

She turns and right by her, in the
shadows, is a man.

Mostly. He is hideously disfigured,
a combination of self-mutilation
and the bubbling red of radiation
poisoning. His clothes are rags,
his eyes pinpoints of glazed madness.

A blade blurs through frame...

**INT. TRADING STATION -
CONTINUING**

River SCREAMS and flops onto her
back, pinned by revelation.
Others look at her, concerned,
as Jayne makes his way
to her.

JAYNE
What the hell is up? You all right?
What's goin' on?

He holds her, as she whispers,
wide-eyed...

RIVER
Reavers.

INT. VAULT - MOMENTS LATER

Zoe is hauling out the last of
five bags as Mal talks to the
guard, holding his gun at him:

MAL
Leg's good, it'll bleed plenty and we avoid any necessary organs...

GUARD
I was thinking more of a graze...

MAL
Well you don't want it to look like you just gave up...

GUARD
No, I get that...

JAYNE (O.S.)
MAL!

MAL
(to himself)
Every heist, he's gotta start yelling my name —

JAYNE
(barreling in)
Mal! Reavers! The girl's pitchin' a fit. They're here or they're comin' soon.

He is already loading up with bags as Mal thinks quickly.

MAL
(to Zoe and Jayne)
Get on the Mule.
(to the guard, pointing to the vault)
Does that open from the inside?

GUARD
Whah -ah- yes...

MAL
You get everyone upstairs in there and you seal it. Long as you got air you don't open up, you understand?

GUARD
I — Buh I —

Mal is in his face, dark and huge:

MAL
GET THEM INSIDE THE VAULT.

EXT. TRADING STATION - DAY

The doors burst open, Jayne and Zoe coming out first, Mal behind with River in hand. She is freaked, in her own space. Jayne and Zoe throw the bags on —

MAL
Zoe take the wheel —

Above: Initial concept for the Trading Station's vault. Production designer Barry Chusid: 'Upstairs it's all dusty and there's a store feeling. When you go down, they've carved out of the ground this vault, where it's much harder materials, colder, very rigid Alliance.'

Below: One of many designs drawn up for a Reaver fighting sword, perfect for the 'up-close kill'.

Below right: Pre-production visualization of the Reaver harpoon hitting Jayne's leg.

JAYNE
You see 'em? Anybody see 'em?

— and jump on themselves, Mal scanning the area as he hands River up to Jayne's care. As the craft powers up, slowly moving, the young man Zoe kept from trying to pull his weapon bursts out of the station, grabbing the back of the Mule.

YOUNG MAN
Take me with you!

MAL
Get in the vault with the others —

YOUNG MAN
I can't stay here! Please!

MAL
It's too many. Drive, Zoe.

A Reaver craft ROARS over their heads. It's nearly the size of Serenity. Torn apart, belching smoke — a welded conglomeration of ruined ships, painted for war. Predator, pure. It disappears over the rooftops.

YOUNG MAN
PLEASE!

MAL
Drive!

Zoe's face is set with unhappy determination as she floors it, shooting out and leaving the young man in the dust.

As they move from him, four Reavers jump out of the shadows and grab the young man. Mal unhesitatingly draws his gun. He

nudges a lever with his thumb and a cartridge pops back.

Mal fires twice. The young man takes both bullets in the chest, slumps down dead.

EXT. THE EDGE OF TOWN - DAY

As the Mule shoots past the last building, we see a skiff shoot out from behind the buildings of the adjacent street, right abreast of our gang.

EXT. THE CENTER OF TOWN - DAY

We see the church as the first ship and an even larger one come to hover over it, Reavers dropping down on cable lines to swarm into it.

A Boot, with metal hooks sticking out of the heel like claws, drops right in front of frame, and the Reaver starts running toward the church as well.

ANGLE: As a woman is dragged screaming inside a dark doorway.
ANGLE: A man comes out of his house with a rifle — and a female Reaver dives at him with impossible speed, tackling him.

EXT. DESERT - CONTINUING

The Mule and the skiff are booking through the rocky terrain. The skiff swings closer, but Jayne peppers it with automatic fire and it swings away. There is sporadic return fire.

JAYNE
How come they ain't blowing us out of the air?

MAL
They wanna run us down. The up-close kill.

River is squashed down on her back, being very small.

RIVER
They want us alive when they eat us.

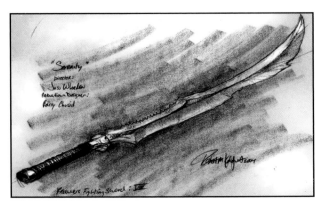

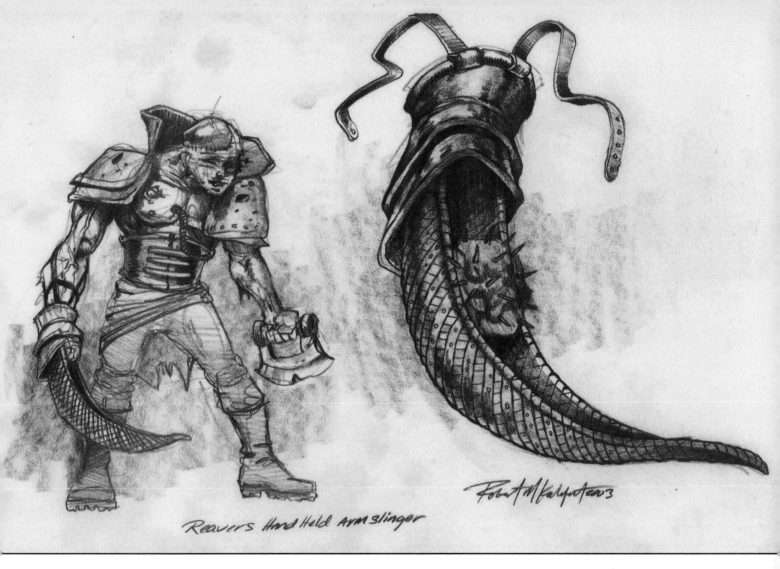

Reavers Hand Held Arm Slinger

JAYNE
Boy, sure would be nice if we had some grenades, don'tchya think?

Mal says nothing, keeps firing.

ZOE
Wash, baby can you hear me?

INT. SERENITY: BRIDGE - CONTINUING

Wash is in a frenzy of switch flipping, prepping for take-off.

WASH
We're moments from air. You got somebody behind you?

We intercut Wash and Zoe at this point:

EXT. DESERT - CONTINUING

ZOE
Reavers.

WASH
(Chinese)
Ai-yah. Tyen-ah...
[English: Merciless hell...]

ZOE
We're not gonna reach you in time.

WASH
Just keep moving, honey. We're coming to you.

EXT. SERENITY - CONTINUING

As she lifts off and starts heading toward the others.

EXT. DESERT - CONTINUING

The Mule rockets over frame followed hard upon by the skiff. A short arrow pins the ammo container shut just as Jayne is going to open it. He tries to pry it loose, stands to get leverage —

A harpoon thwinngs through the air from the skiff and SHHNNK! Goes through Jayne's leg. The harpoon grips the leg and pulls —

Jayne goes flying off the back of the Mule, Mal just grabbing him as the harpoon line reels slowly tighter —

MAL
Grab on!

Jayne grabs the Mule, legs dangling, pulled out between the two vessels as Mal slams a new cartridge into his pistol.

JAYNE
I won't get et! You shoot me if they take me!

Mal steadies himself and takes aim, seemingly at Jayne –

JAYNE
Well don't shoot me first!

Above: Design for another weapon from the Reaver arsenal: the Hand Held Arm Slinger.

THE REAVER SKIFF

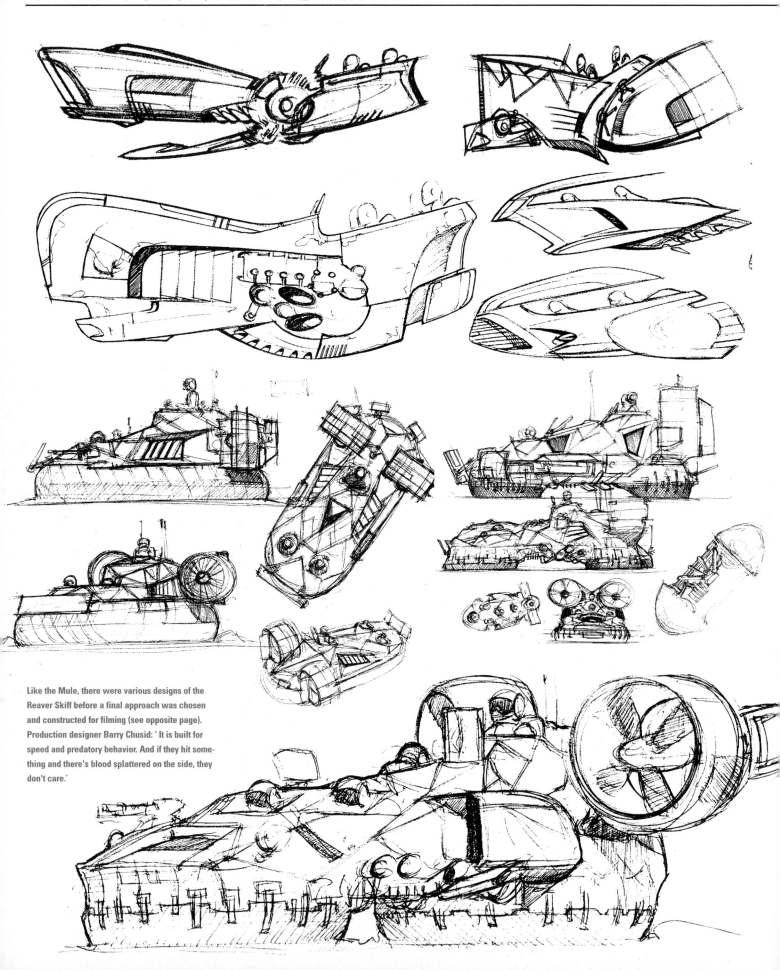

Like the Mule, there were various designs of the Reaver Skiff before a final approach was chosen and constructed for filming (see opposite page). Production designer Barry Chusid: ' It is built for speed and predatory behavior. And if they hit something and there's blood splattered on the side, they don't care.'

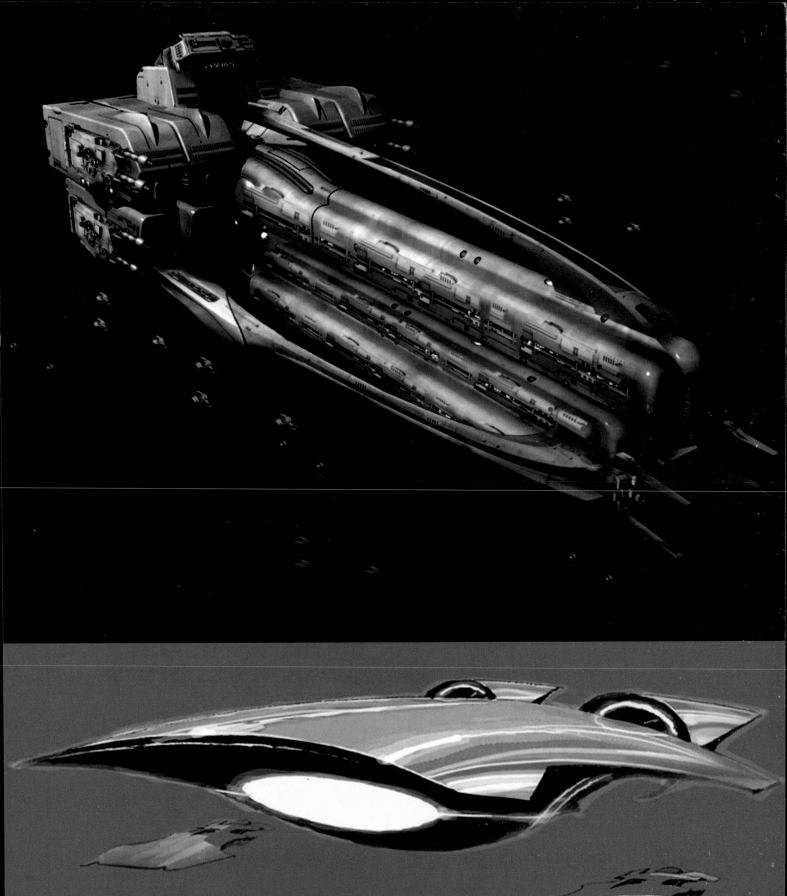

SERENITY 135

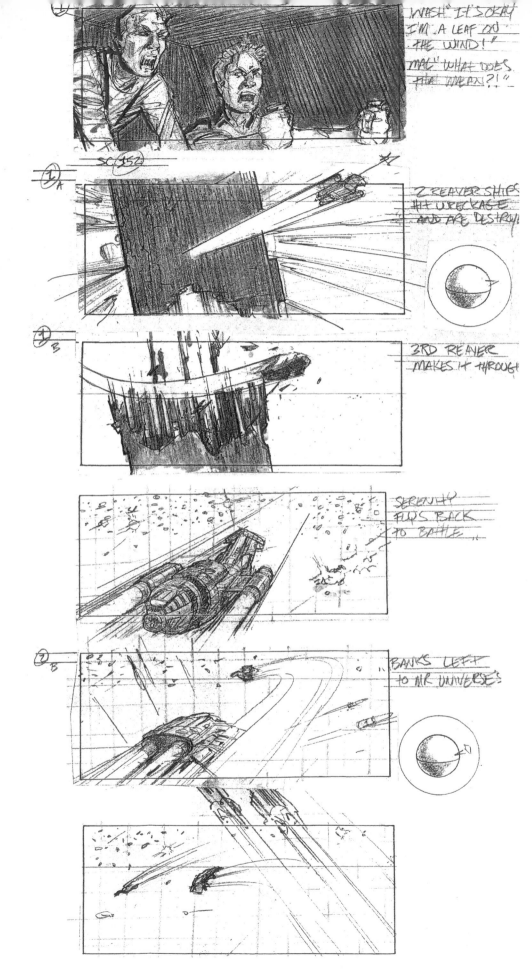

INT. BRIDGE - CONTINUING

Mal looks out at the chaos...

MAL
Chickens come home to roost...
They are suddenly JOLTED by a glancing blow from another ship — Wash struggles to control her —

MAL
The hell —

WASH
(panicky)
It's okay! I am a leaf on the wind!

MAL
(also panicky)
What does that mean?

EXT. SPACE - VFX - CONTINUING

Serenity makes her way past the carnage and heads down toward the tiny satellite moon.

INT. THE OPERATIVE'S SHIP - CORRIDOR - CONTINUING

As the vessel shakes, clearly breached, The Operative runs through the smoky hall. He stops to pull a laser side-arm from a dead soldier. Moves to a pair of doors that open onto standing, almost formfitting one-man cock-pits. The first is open, the blood-ied Ensign trying to get in. The Operative helps him in, puts his hand on the release lever and shuts the door, opens the second and drops in. The door shuts and he yanks his release lever.

EXT. THE OPERATIVE'S SHIP - VFX - CONTINUING

The Dart disengages and bullets down towards the surface. As it moves from the Operative's ship, we see that a Reaver vessel has smashed into the main viewshield, and the ship is spinning, explosions popping silently all over it. The Ensign's dart is only partially disen-gaged when it explodes as well.

EXT. SERENITY - VFX - CONTINUING

She continues down, the metallic expanse of Mr Universe's little moon complex sprawling below them. A moment after Serenity blows through frame, so does a Reaver ship.

It fires an electronic pulse at Serenity and sparks fly.

INT. BRIDGE - CONTINUING

WASH
We're fried! I got no control!

INT. ENGINE ROOM - CONTINUING

Sparks — and arcs of electricity — are everywhere here. Kaylee jumps back as she is electrocuted — Simon runs in and pulls her out, slams the door shut on the erupting fires.

INT. BRIDGE - CONTINUING

MAL
Where's the back up? Where's the back up?

He and Wash are frantically flipping buttons — the ship whirs to a semblance of life —

ZOE
Back up reads at 20%...
(to Wash)
Can you get us down?

WASH
I'm gonna have to glide her in!

ZOE
Will that work?

WASH
Long as that landing strip is made of fluffy pillows...

MAL
(on the com)
Everybody to the upper decks! Strap yourselves to something!

EXT. LANDING STRIP - VFX - CONTINUING

We can see it, a long strip, which halfway along becomes a kind of hangar. Serenity arcs at it uncomfortably fast.

INT. BRIDGE - CONTINUING

Wash is fighting the stick with extreme concentration as Zoe pulls out a seat as well, straps in.

INT. DINING ROOM - CONTINUING

Jayne, Simon and Inara pull harnesses not unlike "Batman the Ride" seats from the ceiling, help the others in.

EXT./INT. LANDING STRIP/HANGAR - VFX - CONTINUING

And Serenity HITS the ground — the landing gear folds and snaps under the weight — the ship keeps going, now inside the hangar, heading towards the entrance to the facility, slowing, fishtailing and coming about a full one-eighty —

Opposite and above: 'Serenity makes her way past the carnage and heads down toward the tiny satellite moon', from storyboard to the final scene.

A standing beam shears off one of the side thrusters –

INT. BRIDGE - CONTINUING

The team are shaken badly —

INT. DINING ROOM - CONTINUING

— as are the rest —

INT. LANDING STRIP - CONTINUING

— she goes beyond the strip and crashes down into the pedestrian area, so that the nose is sticking back out at the runway but the body of the ship is hidden from it.

INT. BRIDGE - CONTINUING

There is a moment of quiet.

WASH
I am a leaf on the wind. Watch —

A massive harpoon CRASHES through the windshield and impales him to his chair. It's as thick around as a telephone pole.

Wash has time to open his mouth in surprise before he is dead.

ZOE
WASH!

She moves to him —

ZOE
Wash baby baby no, come on, you gotta move you gotta move baby please —

Mal rips her away and to the floor as another projectile slams through the window into the wall above them.

EXT. LANDING STRIP - CONTINUING

We see the ship that fired the harpoons as it has entered from an opening in the roof of the hangar. A second Reaver vessel enters frame from above, about to land next to it.

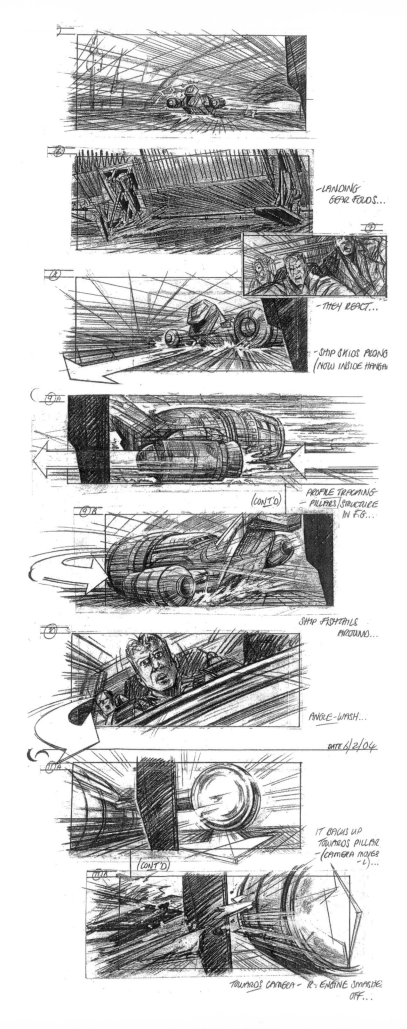

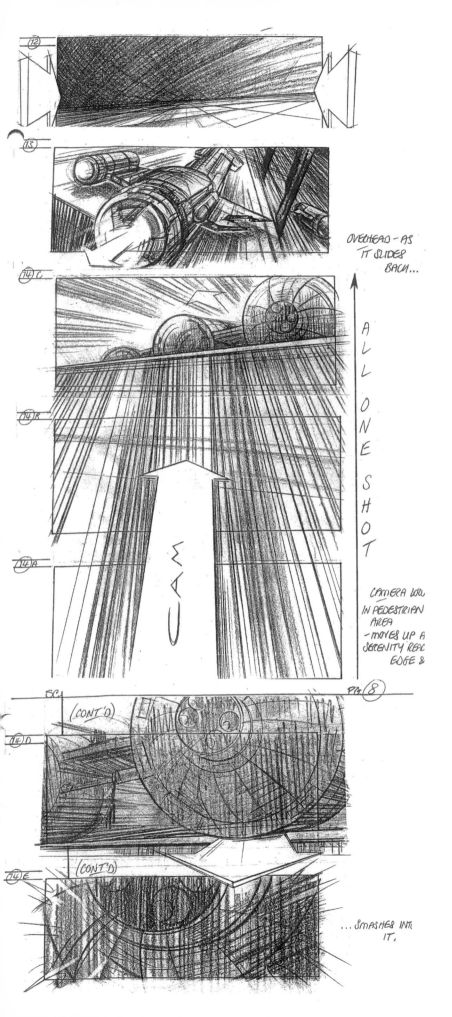

OVERHEAD - AS
IT SLIDES
BACK...

A
L
L

O
N
E

S
H
O
T

CAMERA LOW
IN PEDESTRIAN
AREA
- MOVES UP A
SERENITY REAR
EDGE &

PG (8)

...SMASHES INTO
IT,

EXT. SERENITY - MOMENTS LATER

The cargo bay door opens — just the little door housed inside the ramp — and Jayne comes out with his biggest gun. He looks up, toward the edge of the runway, but no Reavers have arrived yet.

JAYNE
Go!

The entire crew piles out, all heavily bedecked with weapons.

MAL
Head inside!

INT. BLACK ROOM/INNER HALL - MOMENTS LATER

A small double-sized doorway leads to the "Black Room", which is the entrance proper to the facility.

Mal hits a button and huge, thick, blast doors open from the sides AND the top and bottom, creating the effect of a square hole getting bigger. The hall itself is smaller than the black room, but still has the arrows on the ceiling, that point to an elevator some fifty feet away.

MAL
Come on. Jayne, rearguard.

Zoe slows, looking around her.

ZOE
Sir.
(he turns to her)
This is a good hold point.

MAL
We all stay together —

ZOE
No. They have to come through here; they'll bottleneck and we can thin 'em out. We get pushed back there's the blast doors.

KAYLEE
I can rig 'em so they won't re-open once they close.

MAL
Then shut 'em and hide til —

ZOE
We need to draw them til it's done. This is the place. We'll buy you the time.

JAYNE
(to the others)
Move those crates back there for cover — and make sure they ain't filled with anything goes boom.

KAYLEE
Wait, Wash — where's Wash?

Nobody (but River) realized he wasn't there. Zoe is dead calm.

ZOE
He ain't comin'.

Everybody takes that in, Kaylee's eyes welling up.

JAYNE
Move the gorram crates! Come on!

We hear savage SCREAMS from the hanger — they're approaching. Mal moves to the door, Jayne beside him.

ANGLE: HIS POV

Reavers rush toward them. He turns to Jayne.

MAL
Tell me you brought 'em this time...

Jayne smiles grimly, tosses Mal a grenade as he pops his own and fastballs it at the Reavers.

It explodes in their midst, smoke and man-parts flying about. Mal rolls his a shorter distance, then slams the door shut.

ANGLE: THE GRENADE

Explodes, raining a bunch of equipment — and part of a cat-walk — right in front of the door. In the black room, the door nearly buckles from the explosion. Everyone takes positions behind the crates. Zoe stands calmly, her back to the door, loading her sawed-off.

MAL
(continuing; moving back to Zoe)
Zoe... are you here?

She looks up at him.

ZOE
Do the job, sir.

MAL
You hold. Hold till I'm back. He takes off — passes Inara, the two of them holding a look for as long as they can. Then he's in the elevator and gone.

Jayne moves over to Zoe.

JAYNE
Captain's right. Can't be thinking on revenge if we're gonna get through this.

ZOE
You really think any of us are gonna get through this?

He looks back at their army: A companion, a doctor, a mechanic and a more-than-usually out of it River. A beat, and he looks back at Zoe with forlorn hope:

JAYNE
I might...

INT. MR UNIVERSE'S HQ - MOMENTS LATER

The elevator stops and Mal makes his way to the island of screens and machines in the center of the space.

The first thing he takes in is that every broadwave port has been destroyed. The second:

ANGLE: MR UNIVERSE is lying dead, eyes open, half draped on his equally still lovebot. A trail of blood shows he crawled from his chair.

Mal comes close. Nothing. He starts to move away again and the lovebot turns her head, her eyes focusing with an audible whir. She speaks with surprisingly realistic expressiveness, and a warped, computery version of Mr Universe's voice.

LOVEBOT
Mal.

Mal stops.

LOVEBOT
Guy killed me, Mal. He killed me with a sword. How weird is that? I got... a short span here... they destroyed my equipment but I have a back-up unit... bottom of the complex, right over the generator. Hard to get to. I know they missed it. They can't stop the signal, Mal. They can never stop the signal.
(beat)
Okay this is painful. On many levels. I'm not —

She turns back, powering down. Recording over.

A beat, and Mal takes off.

INT. BLACK ROOM - CONTINUING

Inara is on her knees, unwrapping

the oilcloth we saw in her shuttle. River is in the corner, clutching her head.

RIVER
I can't shut them up...

SIMON
It's okay...

RIVER
They're all made up of rage. I can't...

A BANG as a body slams against the door.

Above: Mr Universe lies dead, half draped on his Lovebot Lenore (Nectar Rose).

JEWEL STAITE

Kaylee is flirtatious, sweet, maybe a little naïve but brilliant when it comes to technical machines and all that stuff. She is very friendly, she's very open, very warm, emotional. She wants everybody to get along. I think she instills that family vibe in the crew when things are going really wrong. She's the one that sort of unconsciously reminds people that all we have is each other. She has a special relationship with everybody on board, she doesn't have beefs with anybody, she gets along with everybody, everybody I think trusts her and that's rare. I don't think anybody else has that relationship with the crew. She's trustworthy. I think you can just tell that about her, and she cares a lot, about every single one of them in her own way. Even Jayne.

SIMON
Just stay low. I'm right here.

Jayne moves past them to Zoe, takes position by her.

JAYNE
She picked a sweet bung of a time to go helpless on us.

ZOE
(calls out)
Jayne and I take the first wave. Nobody shoots less they get past our fire.

Simon moves to Kaylee, who is shaky as hell. The bangs on the door continue.

KAYLEE
Oh, I didn't plan on going out like this. I think we did right, but...

SIMON
I never planned... anything. I just wanted to keep River safe. Spent so much time on Serenity trying to find us a home I never realized I already had.

She looks at him with soft surprise.

SIMON
My one true regret in all this is never being with you.

KAYLEE
With me? You mean to say, as, sex?

SIMON
(smiles)
I mean to say.

Kaylee snaps her cartridge home with way more precision than we might expect from her, takes steady aim at the door.

KAYLEE
Hell with this. I'm gonna live.

Simon looks at her a moment, then turns his attention to the door.

Inara come up into frame with the contents of the oilcloth: a bow and arrow, which she pulls back with focused grace.

ANGLE: THE DOOR starts to come off its hinges.

INT. MR UNIVERSE'S HQ - CONTINUING

A panel is kicked in from the ceiling and the Operative drops down, having clearly entered from a different location.

He looks around, carrying a laser-pistol. He moves past Mr Universe and Lenore —

LOVEBOT
Mal.
(The Operative turns)
Guy killed me, Mal.

INT. BASEMENT, OVER THE GENERATOR - CONTINUING

Mal has reached it and surveys the situation.

Before him is a railing, and he can look down on the generator shaft. It's miles deep, with machines rotating and grinding,

and arcs of electricity ricochetting around it.

On the other side is a platform, with the broadwave console sitting behind a clear plastic partition. Cables and chains run along the ceiling, around a series of ladder rungs.

MAL
Hard to get to. That's a fact.

INT. BLACK ROOM - CONTINUING

The door is pried partially open — enough for one Reaver to squeeze through and charge.

Zoe stands up and shoots him in the head. He arcs back hard as the second comes, Zoe shoots him, calmly walking toward the door —

JAYNE
Zoe... Gorramnit...

But she is in a trance, and we see beneath the calm, to the bubbling magma of rage that keeps her firing, single shots, each one a kill,

till five men down and she's out of ammo.

The sixth comes at her swinging a blade and she blocks, the precision of military training still in her as she flips him, wresting the blade free and swinging it down out of frame, bringing it up bloody, swinging again as the door bursts open and she's rushed from behind —

But Jayne totes an automatic, sprays killing fire on the lot, moving forward himself —

JAYNE
ZOE! Get yer ass back in the line!

She looks up, almost confused — and one of Jayne's targets comes back off the ground and slices at her back with a blade, she screams as he cuts deep — and an arrow lodges in his neck.

Inara pulls up a fresh arrow, shaking only slightly.

INT. BASEMENT, OVER THE GENERATOR - LATER

Mal is on the railing, reaching for the 'rungs' on the ceiling just above him. He can almost get them — one wrong move and he pitches into the jaws of death...

A laser shot nails him in the lower back — he arches, legs sliding off the rail — he falls and hits the rail with the backs of his legs, flipping painfully onto his face as he falls, mercifully, back onto the platform.

The Operative comes around some equipment for a closer shot as Mal gets shakily up.

MAL
(in pain)
Shot me in the back. I haven't... made you angry, have I?

THE OPERATIVE
There's a lot of innocent people in the air being killed right now.

MAL
You have no idea how true that is.

There's no wise-ass attitude in him now. They stand, facing off at ten paces.

Above: 'The door is pried partially open — enough for one Reaver to squeeze through and charge.'

Above: Facing the Reavers. Inara's bow and arrow was replaced in post-production by a CG gun.

MAL
I know the secret. The truth that burned up River Tam's brain and set you after her. And the rest of the 'verse is gonna know it too. 'Cause they need to.

THE OPERATIVE
You really believe that?

MAL
I do.

THE OPERATIVE
You willing to die for that belief?

MAL
I am.

The Operative raises his gun — but Mal is the quickdraw master, shoots the gun out of the Operative's hand and gets two hits to the chest (armored) before he makes it to cover.

MAL
Of course, that ain't exactly plan A... He drops out his cartridge and slams another in.

The Operative hides behind some machinery. Tries to peek out at Mal — and more shots send him scrambling back to cover.

Mal holsters his gun and jumps for the rung above him, starts going hand over hand to the island, moving as fast as he can.

The Operative sees his moment, dives for his gun — but it's been ruined by Mal's shot. He looks over at Mal with death in his eyes. He runs at the railing, vaults off it, and grabs a chain — it snaps and he swings, grabbing another.

He reaches Mal and double kicks him from behind — Mal flies off

the rung but grabs a chain — he tries to kick at the Operative, but the guy is frikkin' Tarzan, he climbs up and pulls a lever releasing one end of Mal's chain — Mal goes swinging, smacks into the wall six feet below the platform.

He scrambles up just as the Operative swings himself toward the platform from above.

INT. BLACK ROOM/INNER CORRIDOR - CONTINUING

Jayne is still firing continuously as he drags Zoe back to the barricades. Simon moves to help — Kaylee firing now, squinting with effort — and pulls open the cut back of Zoe's shirt, checks the wound.

SIMON
Spine's intact —

ZOE
Just gimme a bandage.

Simon pulls a spraycan from his bag, sprays the wound with a foam that hardens instantly into an elastic covering.

There are a few gun shots (as well as nail-balls and blades) from the Reavers. Jayne switches weapons, tossing another to Zoe and opening fire —

JAYNE
Oh, now you're likin' guns, huh? Cheaters!

He takes a hit in the shoulder, grimaces and keeps firing.

River watches, the gun limp in her hand. Kaylee grabs it and starts another round — but she's peppered with dart-like projec-

tiles. She screams and drops the weapon, pulling the projectiles from her — Inara helps her up, pulls her back as Zoe shouts:

ZOE
Everybody fall back! Fall back!

Everyone stumbles or is dragged into the inner corridor. Inara hits the controls and the doors start to close, from each side and above and below. Then, when the hole is maybe four by four, they stop.

ZOE
Jayne! Grenade!

JAYNE
Very last one...

He tosses it through the hole. Zoe doesn't even flinch from the

blast as she thinks.

ZOE
They're gonna get in —

KAYLEE
Can close it... from outside...

ZOE
No one's coming back from that...

She tries to stand, fails.

ZOE
How much ammo do we have?

JAYNE
We got three full cartridges and my swingin' cod. That's all.

Inara is by the elevator, pounding for it to come.

INARA
Lift isn't moving...

Below: Designs for the Reavers' dart-like projectiles.

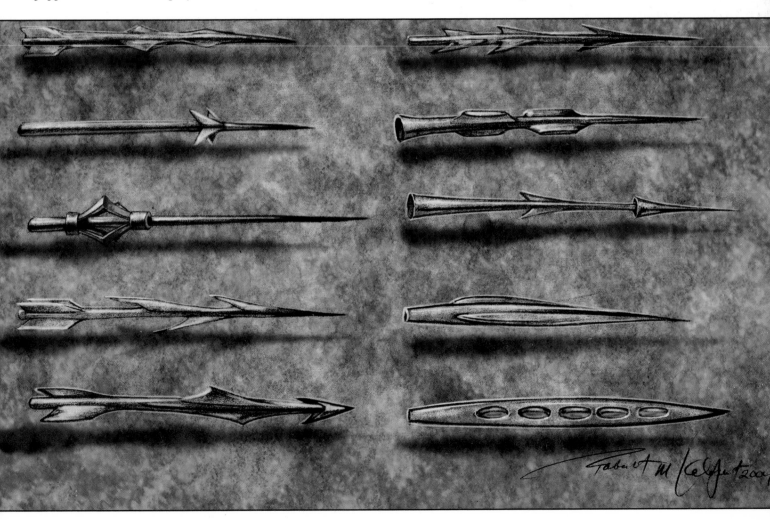

MAKE-UP:
THE REAVERS

The stunning Reaver
make-up, only glimpsed in
brief flashes on screen,
can be seen here in all its
horrific glory.

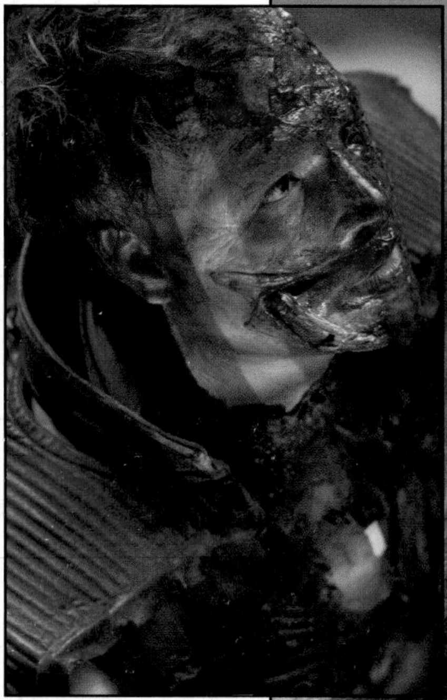

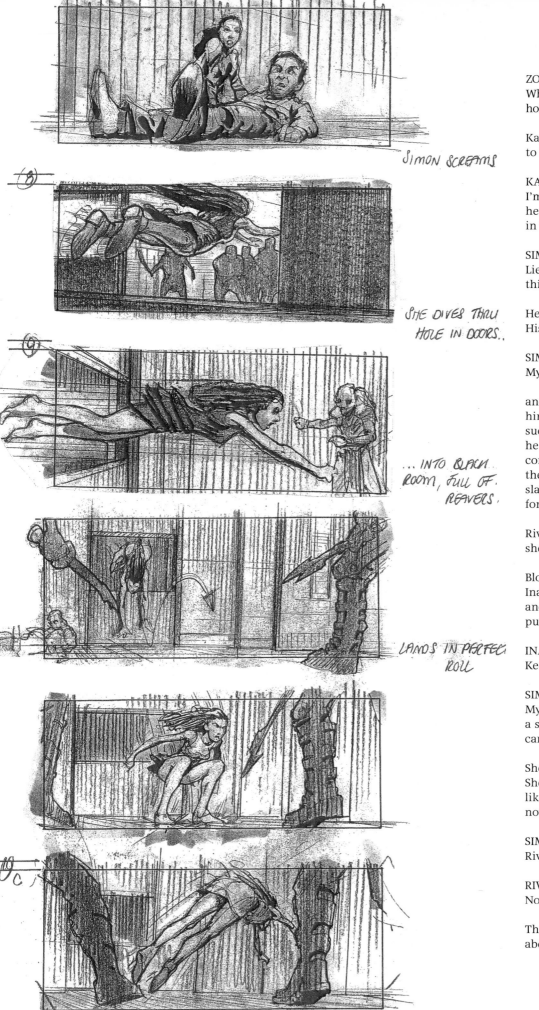

SIMON SCREAMS

SHE DIVES THRU HOLE IN DOORS..

... INTO BLACK ROOM, FULL OF REAVERS.

LANDS IN PERFECT ROLL

ZOE
When they come, try to plug the hole with 'em...

Kaylee cries out and Simon moves to her.

KAYLEE
I'm starting to lose some feeling here... I think there's something in them darts they throwed at me.

SIMON
Lie still. I'm gonna give you something to counteract the —

He stands, looking around him. His bag is over by Zoe.

SIMON
My bag.

and SHKOWW!, the bullet takes him in the belly — everything suddenly moving very slowly as he spins slightly, one foot lifted, a confused expression on his face — then speeding right back up as he slams down on his back, gasping for air.

River's mouth opens in a scream she doesn't make.

Blood spreads from Simon's belly. Inara rushes to him, grabs cloth and puts pressure on the wound, puts Simon's hand on it.

INARA
Keep pressure here...

SIMON
My bag. Need... adrenaline... and a shot of calaphar for Kaylee... I can't... River...?

She is by his side, takes his hand. She has a kind of serenity to her, like she understands something now.

SIMON
River... I'm sorry...

RIVER
No. No.

The lights go out. Everyone looks about them. Jayne fires again, but

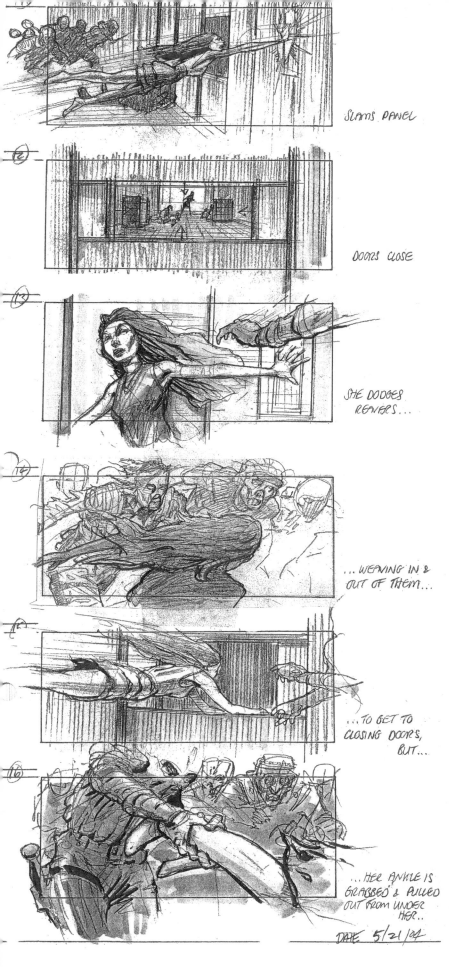

SLAMS PANEL

DOORS CLOSE

SHE DODGES REAVERS...

...WEAVING IN & OUT OF THEM...

...TO GET TO CLOSING DOORS, BUT...

...HER ANKLE IS GRABBED & PULLED OUT FROM UNDER HER..

DATE 5/21/04

all the sound has bled out save these two.

SIMON
I hate to... leave...

RIVER
You won't. You take care of me, Simon. You've always taken care of me.

She stands as the emergency lights come on, giving her face an unearthly glow as she looks down at him.

RIVER
My turn.

She's running so fast, nobody has time to react til she DIVES through the hole in the doors, then Simon SCREAMS her name, the scream following us back into the Black Room where River lands in a perfect roll, comes up in a room full of Reavers.

Without a moment's hesitation she makes it to the panel, gets the doors closing. She dodges a blade, but a blow to the back of the head shakes her. She weaves around a couple of Reavers to get to the closing doors, but at the last second her ankle is grabbed and pulled out from under her.

The last thing we see is her being dragged back as they swarm over her.

ANGLE: THE BLAST DOORS, as they shut with a shuddering KLUNG.

INT. BASEMENT, OVER THE GENERATOR - CONTINUING

Mal gets up the chain to the platform. The Operative is on Mal before he gets his footing, tackles him as Mal's gun goes skittering over the edge into oblivion. There is a railing here or Mal would go over as well — but he comes back with a couple of hammer blows, gets the Operative off him.

They square off, Mal stumbling back into a tool chest, knocking over tools and computer parts.

The Operative reaches behind him and pulls his sword gracefully from the holster under his jacket.

Mal produces his weapon: a tiny screwdriver.

He hurls a toolbox at the Operative and rushes him, gets inside sword range and tries for the neck with the screwdriver — the Operative blocks it and works the sword point against the edge of Mal's stomach. Starts pushing slowly, despite Mal's resistance, and breaks skin.

Mal looks at the Operative a moment — and the sword slides all the way through Mal's belly. Mal's eyes go wide.

THE OPERATIVE
You know what your sin is, Malcolm?

MAL
(shaky smile)
Aw hell, I'm a fan of all seven.

He headbutts the Operative viciously, then punches him so hard he staggers back, losing his grip on the sword. The Operative responds with a spin kick — Mal holds up the screwdriver and the Operative swings his foot right into

it, gasping as Mal pulls the screw-driver — and leg it's stuck in — back as he rockets his fist into the Operative's chin.

The Operative goes down hard, dazed, as Mal grabs the sword still in his belly.

MAL
But right now...

He pulls the sword out, grimacing. Holds it over the Operative. The smile gone.

MAL
I'm gonna have to go with Wrath.

He stabs down at his foe's face — but the Operative rolls out of the way, kicks Mal from the ground and is up in a second, grabbing Mal's sword hand — the sword drops — and punching him repeatedly in his stomach wound.

INT. INNER HALL - CONTINUING

The gang is subdued — because they are all of them injured and Simon is slipping away. Jayne looks at Zoe.

JAYNE
You suppose he got through? Think Mal got the word out?

ZOE
(almost convincingly)
He got through. I know he got through.

INT. BASEMENT, OVER THE GENERATOR - CONTINUING

Mal goes down hard, spitting up blood. He sees the sword, moves — but the Operative kicks him in the face. Picks him up, Mal too tired to throw a decent punch.

THE OPERATIVE
I'm sorry.

The Operative spins him and DIGS his bunched fingers right into the same nerve cluster that he para-lyzed Doctor Mathias with. Mal goes rigid, his face a rictus of pain.

The Operative goes near the railing and retrieves his sword. Mal trem-bles, trying to move — but nothing happens.

THE OPERATIVE
You should know there's no shame in this. You've done remarkable things. But you're fighting a war you've already lost.

He lunges — and Mal twists grace-fully out of the way, grabbing the Operative's swordhand and pulling it forward — while driving his elbow into the Operative's neck with staggering force.

MAL
Well, I'm known for that.

The Operative drops the blade, mouth open, stumbling back, unable to make a sound.

Mal spins him, grabbing both his arms and working his own through them in a twisted full nelson — then bringing his arms up suddenly, the Operative's mouth going wider as we hear his arms crack.

Mal drops him sitting against the railing, picks up his sword, saying:

MAL
Piece a shrapnel tore up that nerve cluster my first tour. Had it moved.

He squats down, looks the Operative in the face.

MAL
Sorry 'bout the throat. Expect you'd wanna say your famous last words now. Just one trouble.

He reaches over the railing, pulls the back of the Operative's jacket through and shoves the sword through the fabric, pinning the Operative in his sitting position.

MAL
I ain't gonna kill you.

He moves to the console, starts prepping it.

MAL
Hell, I'm gonna grant your greatest wish.

He inserts the disc, turns it slightly. It hums to life.

MAL
I'm gonna show you a world without sin.

He hits "send all". The cylinder lights up and the broadcast begins. Here it is projected as a two-dimensional image on the clear plastic partition, right in front of the Operative.

There are images first of the city — of bodies, on the street, in homes and offices.... image after image, just as we saw on the research vessel — and in River's mind.

CARON (V.O.)
These are some of the first sites we scouted on Miranda. There is no one living on this planet. There is no one...

Mal hits the controls and a ramp extends towards the other side. He begins to cross. Never even looks back.

On the Operative, trapped, watching in growing horror...

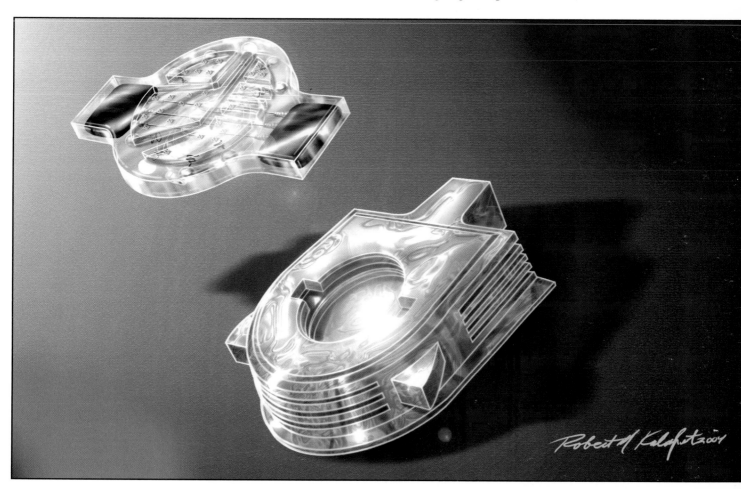

INT. BLACK ROOM - CONTINUING

CLOSE ON: A Reaver in EXTREME SLOW MOTION. Face full of fury, he is swinging his blade in a frenzy of hate.

And a small hand smashes that face so hard that teeth fly — the Reaver clearing frame to reveal:

River.

She is bloodied, but not killed. She's as she was in the bar — moving faster and more efficiently than anyone can, ducking and weaving and gutting and kicking and there are piles of Reavers already, she never breaks concentration as she uses their own blades against them, throws them, does everything in her power to stay one step ahead of — or above — the mob.

She slams backwards into a wall opposite the blast doors — and a grappling hook punches through it, just missing her.

INT. BASEMENT, OVER THE GENERATOR - CONTINUING

The Operative watches the end of the broadcast. We are on his face through the clear plastic, so the images projected on it blur right before him: the Reaver, Dr. Caron — and her screaming doesn't stop til something is shoved in her mouth.

INT. INNER HALL - CONTINUING

The gang is still trying to patch themselves together when the elevator doors open. Mal staggers out, holding his bleeding side.

ZOE
Sir?

MAL
It's done. Report?

Zoe looks at the badly wounded Simon, is about to give a report — and the doors start to open behind her.

Everyone turns to look, those who can feebly raising weapons, as the square iris of the opening blast doors widens to reveal River, standing alone. She is holding two Reaver blades, is bloody but unbowed. And the only one alive.

We hold on her a moment, then the wall behind her is ripped completely away.

Behind it, grappling hooks chained to a huge tractor pull the wall away as through the smoke come some fifteen Alliance soldiers, who line up, rifles trained on our gang...

SOLDIER
Drop your weapons! Drop 'em now!

ANOTHER SOLDIER
Do we engage? Do we engage?

Mal and the others tense up. River turns slowly to face the soldiers, blades still gripped... A soldier levels his gun at her, sweaty and frantic... others still shouting...

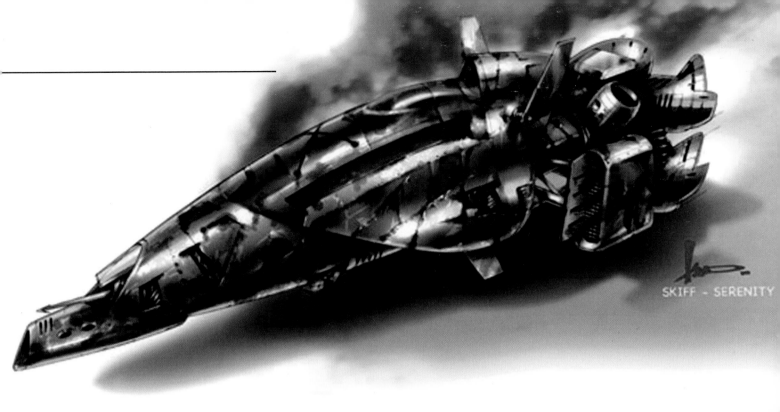

SKIFF - SERENITY

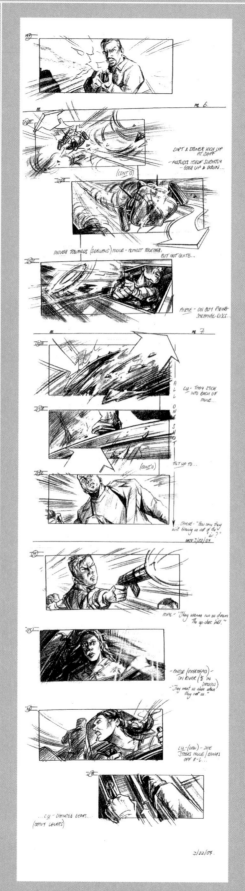

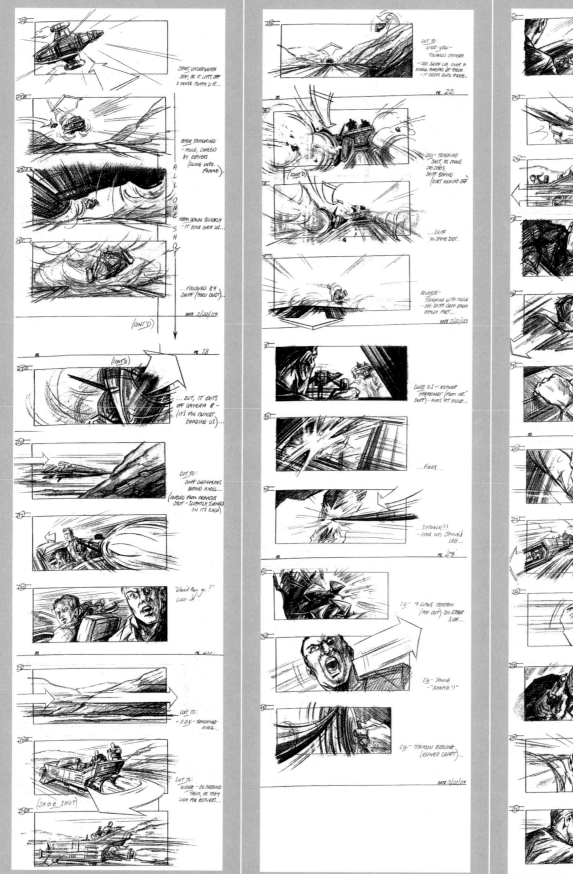

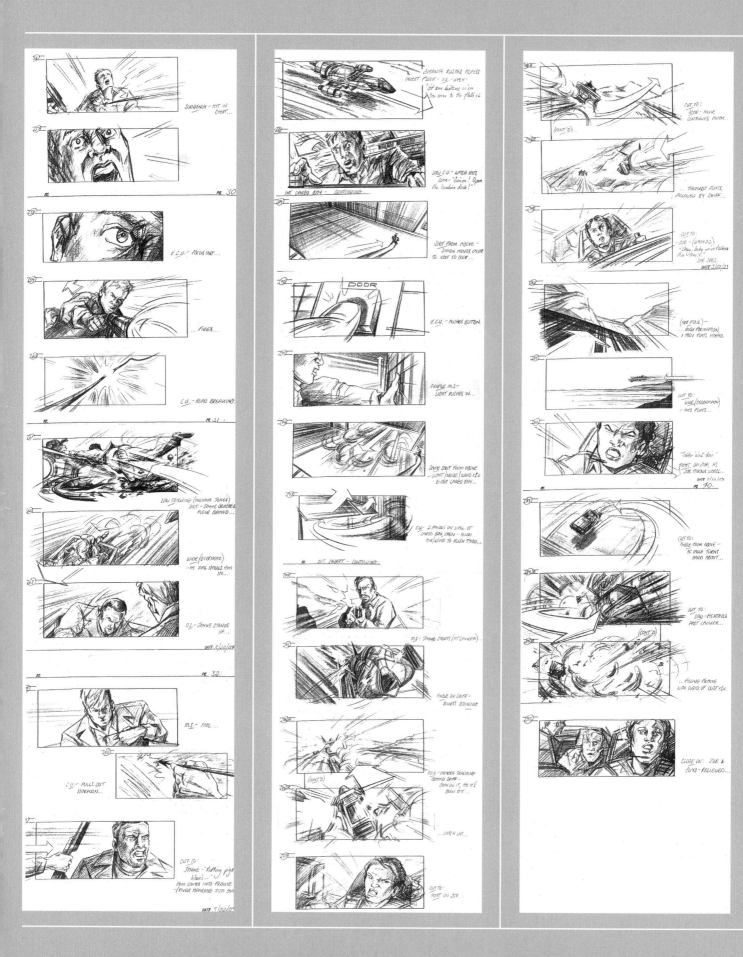

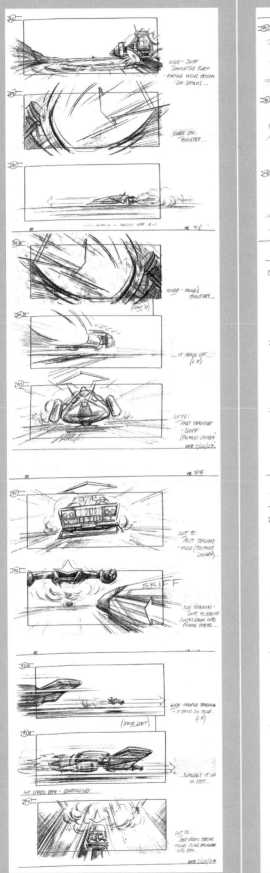

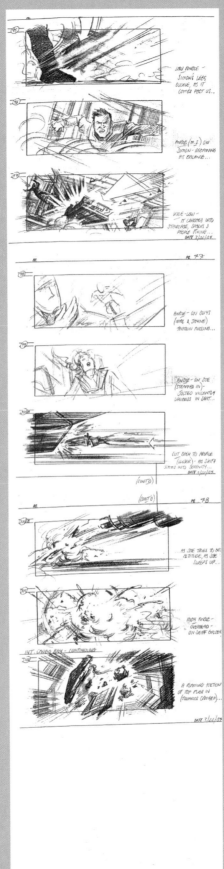

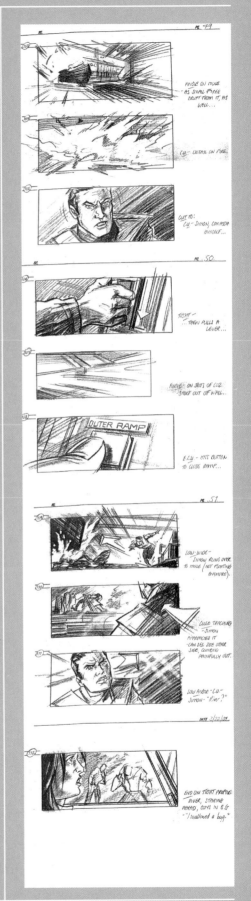

Above: The Barn Swallow.
The Mule crashes back-
wards into the cargo bay.

Mal fires. Again. Steadies himself for one more...

The line holding the harpoon is split by Mal's third shot.

The Mule surges forward as Jayne drags on the ground. Mal hauls him in as River bounds into the front to make room.

JAYNE
Rutting pigs! Where's —

And River is holding out his weapon before he can ask for it.

EXT. ANOTHER PART OF THE DESERT - CONTINUING

Serenity rushes across the desert floor, not much higher off it than the smaller crafts.

INT. BRIDGE - CONTINUING

WASH
(to Zoe)
Get some distance on 'em. You come to the flats, I want you to

swing round. Gonna try a Barn Swallow.

Wash hits the com.

WASH
Simon! Open her up!

INT. CARGO BAY - CONTINUING

Simon is next to the huge sliding doors at the front, hits a couple of buttons. The doors pull open, as the huge ramp beyond them opens down, letting in a rush of wind and light.

EXT. DESERT - CONTINUING

Zoe sees the flats ahead. She veers into some rocks, breaking them loose. The rocks bounce at the skiff and hit an engine, forcing it to veer behind a rise.

EXT. DESERT FLATS - CONTINUING

The Mule reaches the flats, away from the rocks.

WASH (O.S.)
(in Zoe's ear)
Okay, baby, we've talked this through...

ZOE
Talkin' ain't doin'.

The skiff reappears, far behind but coming fast. Zoe throws the wheel and the Mule comes hard about, fishtailing slightly as it faces the oncoming skiff.

WASH (O.S.)
Don't slow down!

ANGLE: THE SKIFF

As it heads for the Mule —

ANGLE: THE MULE

As it heads for the skiff — and Serenity swoops down out of the sky, bay doors open, and comes right up behind it — The Mule swallowed by the bigger ship —

INT. CARGO BAY - CONTINUING

And only its forward momentum keeps it from being squashed as it flies backwards into the bay, narrowly missing Simon and smashing back into the staircase, sparks and people flying —

EXT. DESERT - CONTINUING

Serenity tries to get altitude — but slams right into the oncoming skiff, tearing it apart —

INT. CARGO BAY - CONTINUING

A flaming portion of the top flies in, skids to the floor as small fires erupt from the Mule as well — Simon pulls a lever and jets of CO_2 shoot out of the floor.

Simon hits the button to start the outer ramp closing, then runs to the Mule. The CO_2 stops and he finds River sitting in her seat, completely unharmed. Zoe is climbing painfully out of the other seat, Mal and Jayne both having been thrown.

SIMON
River?

RIVER
I swallowed a bug.

Kaylee runs in to see how everyone is. She goes to Simon.

KAYLEE
Are you okay?

MAL
Is he okay?

A bloodied Reaver POPS into frame from under the skiff-top. He lunges for Mal, baring sharpened teeth —

Mal spins and draws, fires into his belly as Jayne and Zoe both fire at the same time. The freak takes too long to go down, but down he goes. Dies sitting against the skiff top. Everybody takes a moment to look at each other.

WASH (O.S.)
We all here? What's going on? Hello?

ZOE
(moves to the com)
No casualties. Anybody following?

INT. BRIDGE - CONTINUING

WASH
Nice flying, baby, and that's a negative. Clean getaway — Out of atmo in six minutes.

INT. CARGO BAY - CONTINUING

MAL
Set course for Beaumonde.
(to the others)
First thing, I want this bod —

Simon suddenly punches him in the face, causing Mal to stumble back, and Simon to shake his hand in pain.

MAL
(continuing; Chinese)
Nee TZAO ss-MA? Nee-YOW wuh-KAI CHANG?
[English: You wanna bullet? You wanna bullet right in your throat?]

SIMON
You stupid, selfish, son of a whore —

MAL
I'm a hair's breadth from riddling you with holes, Doctor —

SIMON
"One simple job! She'll be fine!"

MAL
She IS fine! Except for bein' still crazy, she's the picture of health!

Below: 'A bloodied Reaver POPS into frame...'

ZOE
Wasn't for River, we'd probably be left there. She felt 'em coming.

SIMON
Never again. You understand me?

MAL
Seems I remember a talk about you giving orders on my boat.

SIMON
Well sleep easy 'cause we're off your boat. Just as soon as River gets her share of the "bounty".

KAYLEE
Well let's not do anything hasty...

MAL
No, shiny! I'm sick a' carrying tourists anyhow. We'll be on Beaumonde in ten hours time, you can pick up your earnings and be on your merry. Meantime you do your job. Patch up my crew.

A beat.

RIVER
He didn't lie down. They never lie down.

She is looking at the Reaver. Everyone does, for a moment.

INT. FOREDECK HALL - MOMENTS LATER

Mal and Zoe enter from below.

ZOE
No, I think things'll glide a deal smoother for us without River and Simon on board... but how long do you think they'll last?

MAL
Doc made his call. They's as babes in a basket when we took 'em in; we sheltered 'em plenty. Man has to cut loose, learn to stand on his own.

ZOE
Like that man back in town?

They stop by Mal's room.

MAL
I had to shoot him. What the

Reavers woulda done to him before they killed him...

ZOE
I know. That was a piece a' mercy. But before that, him begging us to bring him along...

MAL
We couldn't take the weight. Woulda slowed us down.

ZOE
You know that for certain —

MAL
Mule won't run with five. I shoulda dumped the girl? Or you? Or Jayne?
(considering)
Well, Jayne...

ZOE
Coulda tossed the payload.

MAL
And go to Fanty and Mingo with air in our mitts, tell 'em "here's your share"? They'd set the dogs on us in the space of a twitch, and there we are back in mortal peril. We get a job, we gotta make good.

Wash enters from the bridge.

ZOE
Sir, I don't disagree on any particular point, it's just...
in the time of war, we woulda never left a man stranded.

MAL
Maybe that's why we lost.

She's not happy with the reply. Mal climbs down to his room as Wash reaches Zoe, slides his arms around her. She nestles into him...

INT. MAL'S ROOM - CONTINUING

Once alone, Mal lets his own disappointment show. He pulls off his holster and drops it over a chair. Kicks the toilet closed and sits on his bunk.

The place resembles a submarine cabin, with charts and clutter, ancient maps on the walls. Mal

moves a bunch of papers off his bunk and a picture slides out. Hits the floor and starts moving: it's a snapshot-movie of:

INT. INARA'S SHUTTLE - DAY

We're close on a beautiful woman who looks at us with amused exasperation. Behind her is an opulently dressed little shuttle.

INARA
Kaylee, are you ever gonna put that capture down?

KAYLEE (O.S.)
We gotta have records of everything. A bona fide Companion entertained clients on this very ship! In this very bed!

The picture pans over to the bed — which River is bending over and sniffing curiously. Inara is packing things up.

KAYLEE (O.S.)
For one sweet second, we was almost classy.

INARA
You promised to help me pack.

KAYLEE (O.S.)
Honest, Inara, why do you have to leave?

Inara shoots an uncertain look at the camera — and the picture freezes, goes back to the beginning. During all this, Mal has picked it up. He looks at it a moment, tosses it aside. Looks around at nothing much.

GINA TORRES

Zoe serves two masters and yet none at all. It's very interesting. How she gets away with it, I don't know. There's her great love, which is her husband, and there is her great... I want to say passion, but people would probably infer things to that... Zoe's passion really is, I guess, to keep this ship from falling into oblivion. She knows where she's going. She's that career soldier. She is completely loyal to Mal, which can sometimes cause a little friction between she and her husband. But she has an innate understanding of right and wrong.

Below: Kaywinnet Lee Frye, as sweet and cheerful as she is mechanical.

JAYNE (V.O.)
I do not get it. How's a guy get so wrong?

INT. CARGO BAY - LATER

We see the doors in the floor slide open, a second set below. Pan to see, for a moment, the dead Reaver's face.

Kaylee is opening the doors with a keypad on a cable. Jayne drags the corpse closer to the doors as he continues:

JAYNE
Ain't logical. Cuttin' on his own face, rapin' and murdering — I mean, I'll kill a man in a fair fight... or if I think he's gonna start a fair fight, or if he bothers me, or if there's a woman, or I'm gettin' paid — mostly only when I'm gettin' paid. But these Reavers... last ten years they just show up like the bogeyman from stories. Eating people alive? Where does that get fun?

He dumps the body in, she starts the doors closing.

KAYLEE
Shepherd Book said they was men that reached the edge of space, saw a vasty nothingness and just went bibbledy over it.

JAYNE
Hell, I been to the edge. Just looked like more space.

KAYLEE
I don't know. People get awful lonely in the black. Like to get addlepated ourselves, we stay on this boat much longer. Captain'll drive us all off, one by one.

JAYNE
You're just in a whinge cuz that prissy doc is finally disembarking. Me I says good riddance. He never belonged here, and his sister's no saner than one of them Reavers.

ANGLE: RIVER is up on the cat-walk, secretly watching them.

KAYLEE
That ain't even so! River's a dear heart and a boon to this crew! You just don't like her 'cause she can read your mind and everything you think is mean.

JAYNE
Well, there is that.

KAYLEE
Her and Simon could have a place here. Now they're leaving us. Just like Shepherd Book.

She looks up toward one of the shuttles.

KAYLEE
Just like Inara...

INT. COMPANION TRAINING HOUSE - DAY

And here she is, moving back and down into frame, her eyes half closed in passion. She settles on a cluster of brocaded pillows, and we see another head lowering in for a kiss...

Come around to see it's another lovely young woman — and that

there is a group of ten others watching intently, all in saris, on their knees. Two handsome young men with shaved heads in the back, also on their knees.

Inara stops before the kiss, smiling and coming back up. She speaks to the girls (We hear only soft music) as she repositions the one she's with, lowering again; showing her the motion of surrender as if it were a dance step.

A WOMAN'S VOICE (V.O.)
They love you.

EXT. COMPANION TRAINING HOUSE - DUSK

Inara looks out at the mountains. The space she's in resembles a Tibetan monastery, if slightly more opulent.

Widen to see she is with SHEYDRA, a somewhat older Companion, the woman whose voice we heard. She hands Inara a drink.

Above: A scene edited from the theatrical release: Inara and Sheydra at the Companion Training House.

Left: Inara's fellow Companion, Sheydra (Kim Meyers).

THE TRAINING HOUSE

The Companion Training House, set high in the mountains, is described in the script as resembling 'a Tibetan monastery, if slightly more opulent.' Production designer Barry Chusid adds, ['We went for] bright blues, reds, purples; water; screens so things are hidden and then pop out. It's a romantic feeling. You think, "Wow, I could sit there and soak it up for a while."'

This page and opposite page: Concept art for the exterior and interior of the Companion Training House.

Above: Concept art of a Beaumonde street scene.

SHEYDRA
The girls. They've learned more from you these last months than the rest of us could show them in two years.

INARA
They're very sweet. But they're not Companions.

INT. COMPANION TRAINING HOUSE - DAY

As they talk, we see a couple more quick flashes of life in the house.

From above, we see Inara walking amongst a group of girls practicing calligraphy on sheets of parchment laid out on the floor.

SHEYDRA (V.O.)
(wryly)
You've no hope for them? Junk the lot, start anew?

EXT. COMPANION TRAINING HOUSE - DAY

INARA
On Sihnon we started training at twelve. Years of discipline and preparation before the physical act of pleasure was even mentioned. Most of these girls -

INT. COMPANION TRAINING HOUSE - DAY

Inara adjusts a girl's bowmanship, as two more behind her practice theirs — all with no arrows.

SHEYDRA (V.O.)
They're all of good family, the highest academic standards —

INARA (V.O.)
Control.

EXT. COMPANION TRAINING HOUSE - DAY

INARA
Was the first lesson. And the last and these worlds are not like the

Central Planets. There is barbarism dressed up in the most civil weeds. Men of the highest rank who don't know the difference between a Companion and a common whore. It's unsafe.

SHEYDRA
All the more reason the girls look to you. You came out here alone, before the Alliance ever thought to establish a House this remote. You've seen so much. You're a figure of great romance to them.

INARA
Great romance has nothing to do with being a Companion, Sheydra. You should know better.

SHEYDRA
I'm not the one who had a torrid affair with a pirate.

Inara nearly spills her drink.

INARA
A who? With a what?

SHEYDRA
(smiling)
It's the talk of the House. The girls all trade stories in the dorms at night.

INARA
I didn't... have a pirate...

SHEYDRA
In one of the stories you make love in a burning temple. I think that's my favorite.

INARA
(sitting)
This is unbearable. Captain Reynolds is no pirate; he's a petty thief. And he never laid a finger on me. All he ever did was rent me a shuttle and be very annoying.
(Chinese)
Byen dahTAHmenduhBAY joGOluh.
[English: A switch to those girls' back-sides is just good enough.]

SHEYDRA
A year on his shuttle and he never

laid a finger on you. No wonder you left.

INARA
(bridling)
I left because — go away. We're no longer friends. You're a stranger to me now.

SHEYDRA
I do love to watch you boil. Don't worry. The stories will fade. And your Captain Reynolds has probably gotten himself blown up by this time.

INARA
(looking away again)
Yes. That would be just like him.

EXT. BEAUMONDE: ATOLL PLAZA - EVENING

Serenity touches down on the crowded atoll amidst a number of other, equally disreputable ships. The place is filled with every kind of immigrant culture and shop imaginable.

Among the various vignettes we briefly capture is a very proper Asian woman walking by a slovenly Caucasian, who call out to her in Chinese:

MAN
(Chinese)
PEOW-liang de shaojie, nee GOO

wuo HUHnee SHANG-hao. Wuh HWAY wrongnee shungkai roo hua...
[English: Pretty lady, hire me for the night and I'll open you like a flower...]

LADY
(Chinese)
Wuo DWAY-nee BOO-woon, boo-JEN...
[English: I neither see nor hear you...]

EXT./INT. SERENITY - EVENING

The ramp is open and everyone is filing out, ready to hit the town. Kaylee is talking to Simon, who has River in hand.

KAYLEE
Don't talk to the barkers — only the captains. You look the captain in the eye, know who you're dealing with.

SIMON
I wish there was...

Mal passes between them, paying no heed to their moment. We follow him to see the others ahead, the same disreputable man accosting Zoe:

MAN
(Chinese)
PEOW-liang de shaojie, Booleetah, GOOwo...
[English: Pretty lady, forget him and hire me...]

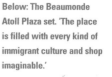

Above: The Maidenhead set.

WASH
(Chinese)
Wo TAI-TAI boo PEOW-liang!
[English: My wife is not pretty!]

Kaylee looks Simon over one last time...

KAYLEE
You shouldn't oughta be so clean. It's a dead giveaway you don't belong, you always gotta be tidy. Don't pay anybody in advance. And don't ride in anything with a Capissen 38 engine, they fall right out of the sky.

SIMON
Kaylee.

She turns and heads off. Simon starts in the other direction, but River looks after her and the others.

SIMON
River... do you want to stay with them?

RIVER
It's not safe.

SIMON
No, I fear it's not safe anymore.

He's heading off and doesn't hear:

RIVER
For them.

**INT. THE MAIDENHEAD -
CONTINUING**

We start on a CorVue screen, showing a news report. On the screen is a shot of the town our gang robbed, now half of it a smoking ruin.

NEWSPERSON (V.O.)
... that it was a band of Reavers remains unconfirmed. The only survivors of the massacre apparently locked themselves in the Trade Station vault until —

During this we come around to see that the screen has a blinking light behind it, come THROUGH the wiring of the back to look out at the bar, with the word "recording" in the corner. Every screen is a camera, even down here.

We pick up Mal and Kaylee heading down into the bar. Cutting away from the camera's view, we can look two stories straight down as they go, to a close group of dark tables and booths and a second screen playing in the corner.

MAL
It's not my fault the Doc's got no stomach for Rim living —

KAYLEE
It is entirely and for all your fault! If you'd given Simon a moment, just a moment where he didn't think you were gonna throw them off or turn them in, he might've —

MAL
What? Swept you into his cleanly arms? Made tidy love to you?

They have reached the guncheck, where Jayne and Wash have already checked their guns. It works like a lunch automat: Mal sticks his gun in a drawer, pulls out a chit — the drawer closes and rotates, revealing another empty one. A large bouncer with a shockrod watches impassively.

KAYLEE
(as they continue down)
Don't you dare joke! You know how much I pined on Simon. And him fair sweet on me, I well believe, but he's so worried about being found out –

ZOE
Captain didn't make 'em fugitives.

KAYLEE
But he coulda made 'em family! Steada driving them off. Steada keeping Simon from seein' I was there, when I carried such a torch and we coulda — goin' on a year now I ain't had nothin' twixt my nethers weren't run on batteries!

MAL
Oh god! I can't know that!

JAYNE
I could stand to hear a little more...

KAYLEE
If you had a care for anybody's heart you woulda —

MAL
(enough)
You knew he was gonna leave. We never been but a way station to those two. And how do you know what he feels? He's got River to worry on but he still coulda shown you... if I truly wanted someone bad enough, wouldn't be a thing in the 'verse could stop me from going to her.

KAYLEE
Tell that to Inara.

For a moment, Mal is too shocked to react. Kaylee storms out.

MINGO
Domestic troubles?

MINGO is young, tough — somewhere between a gangster and a fur-trader. Sounds lower-class British, or something like it.

FANTY
Domestic troubles?

FANTY moves out from behind Mingo to reveal that he is Mingo's identical twin. Apart from slight differences in dress, they are indistinguishable.

MINGO
'Cause we don't wanna interrupt.

FANTY
A man should keep his house in order.

MAL
(greets them each)
Mingo. Fanty.

MINGO
(pointing at his brother)
He's Mingo.

MAL
He's Fanty. You're Mingo.

Below: entering the bar. Production designer Barry Chusid: '[Joss] wanted the feeling you were coming through this small space. You would come in and you would almost get this sense of vertigo looking down.'

MINGO
Ghahh! How is it you always know?

MAL
Fanty's prettier.
(pulling out a chair)
Feel to do some business?

MINGO
(re: Mal's gang)
Bit crowded, isn't it? As you see, we
come unencumbered by thugs.

MAL
Which means at least four of the
guys already in here are yours. All's
one. I'll just keep Jayne with me.

ZOE
Sir, are you sure you don't —

MAL
Go. Go get yourselves a nice romantic meal.

WASH
Those are my two favorite words!
(to Zoe)
Honey... "Meal..."

MAL
(to Zoe)
It's business. We're fine.

They leave and the four remaining men sit. Fanty tosses a few coins to a saloon-girl, who does a little fan-dance...

ANGLE: THE CORVUE CAMERA'S POV of the men is conveniently blocked by her little dance.

Mal's foot nudges a duffel bag of money to Mingo's foot.

MINGO
Quite a crew you've got.

MAL
Yeah, they're a fine bunch of ruebens.

MINGO
How you keep them on that crap boat is the subject of much musing tween me and Fanty.

FANTY
We go on and on.

MAL
So I'm noticing. Is there a problem I don't know of? You got 25% of a sweet take kissing your foot, how come we're not dispersing?

FANTY
Our end is forty, precious.

JAYNE
My muscular buttocks it's forty —

MINGO
It is as of now. Find anyone around going cheaper.

FANTY
Find anyone around going near a sorry lot like you in the first instance.

ANGLE: RIVER has entered, is looking about.

Jayne sees her, nudges Mal, who looks and turns back to business. We stay on her as she wanders around the perimeter of the bar, vaguely listening in on Mal's deal.

FANTY
You're unpredictable, Mal. Which is the single worst thing to be in this business. Mingo and me, we's greedy. Could set your watch by our greed; it wavers never. But you... you run when you oughta fight, fight when you oughta deal. Makes a business person twitchy.

MINGO
Adding in the fact that your ship's older than the starting point of time and you can see you's charity cases to the likes of us.

MAL
Well here's a foul thought. I conjured you two were incompetent; sent us out not knowing there were Reavers about. Now I'm thinking you picked us out because you did.

MINGO
That were a sign of faith, boy. And it doesn't affect our forty per. Danger is, after all, your business.

Above: Artwork used in the anime-style Fruity Oaty Bar commercial.

JAYNE
Reavers ain't business, double dickless.

This is all background noise to River, who has moved to the CV screen, on which is a commercial. It's animated, goofy, cartoon animals and anime-style Asian girls all transforming to insane fantasy figures as they sing about:

COMMERCIAL
FRUITY OATY BARS, POW! HEY! FRUITY BARS, MAKE A MAN OF A MOUSE, MAKE YOU BUST OUT YOUR BLOUSE, EAT THEM NOW, BANG! PING! ZOW! — TRY FRUITY, OATY BARS.

We push in, the light from the CV on River's face, pushing to EXTREME CLOSE UP, all noise but the jingle fading out, finally that as well, just the hum in River's ears.

And she whispers:

RIVER
Miranda.

She turns and looks back at the crowd.

ANGLE: her jacket, as it slips to the floor.

What happens next happens very fast.

She strides silently to the first table — two men drinking quietly — and she slams her foot into one's face, then whips it back into the other's, knocking them both unconscious as —
— people are turning, just registering that this girl —

— kicks the table into a card player even as she sweeps a bottle off it behind her — the bottle hits a man behind her square in the face, a man she never even looked at — people are rising, fleeing or pushing forward —

MAL
River...

JAYNE
Whuhuh?

She's taking out a group of four, high kicks and perfect precision — Two men come from either side, one whipping out a knife — she does a perfect split, grabs his wrist above her head, using his momentum to stab the other one — The bouncer reaches her and she wrests his shockrod from him, uses it on him, on the three men who

cluster in front of Fanty and Mingo like secret service — the fan-dancer is bolting and River hurls the rod at her head, knocks her cold...

ANGLE: Mal and Jayne as the look past the fan dancer.

JAYNE
(continuing; excited)
Hey! A tussle!

MAL
(quietly)
Jayne...

JAYNE
River.

FANTY
You know that girl?

MAL
(still watching)
I really don't.

Mal hands the money to Fanty and Mingo.

MAL
Get out.

MINGO
(as they bolt)
Don't tell us what to do.

She's everywhere. On tables, chairs, under your legs, using the room itself to take out every single person there. One man hides behind a wall — impossibly, she swings her leg around the corner and nails his face.

Jayne grabs her from behind —

JAYNE
Gorrammit, girl, it's me!

She grabs his crotch and squeezes — his grip loosens and she spins, facing him, and flat-heels his nose with her palm, twirling into a gut kick that doubles him over, dispatching of another while she cracks Jayne's head with a small table —

Somebody pulls a gun and she snaps his elbow, causing him to scream out even before he shoots himself in the gut —

Mal frantically wrests a gun from the vending locker as River knocks the other guy's gun in the air, kicks someone else and then catches it, whips it around just as Mal comes up with his, they are pointed right at each other —

SIMON
Eta Kooram Nah Smech!

And River drops to the ground, fast asleep.

There is a beat. Mal looks around the bar. He and Simon, who has run up to the entrance, are the only ones standing.

He looks down at River. She lies unconscious, helpless.

MAL
I think maybe we ought to leave.

EXT. SPACE - VFX - NIGHT

We see two sleek warships glide silently into frame, followed by a third, bigger ship. This is the Operative's vessel, and it is everything Serenity is not: sleek, predatory, icy cool.

INT. THE OPERATIVE'S SHIP - BRIDGE - CONTINUING

The Operative is looking at the Maidenhead security feed — and River is staring right at him.

THE OPERATIVE
(captivated)
Hello again. Yes, it's me. I'm glad you've finally asked for me.

An Ensign is revealed looking at a separate monitor:

ENSIGN
We got a pos on a retinal — man carrying her out is Malcolm Reynolds, captains a Firefly-class transport ship, "Serenity". Bound by law five times, smuggling, tariff dodge... not convicted. Nothing here that would —

PRODUCTION DESIGN:
SHIPS OF THE 'VERSE

A selection of the various craft designed for the film. This page: Two Alliance ships. Opposite page: A freighter (top) and a police vehicle (bottom).

THE OPERATIVE
The ship. The name of the ship.
(softly)
Crossref. Malcolm Reynolds.
Serenity.

He looks over at the Ensign with a small, strange smile on his lips — as his glasses are covered by text.

ENSIGN
Sir?

THE OPERATIVE
Serenity Valley. Bloodiest battle of the entire war. The Independents held the valley for seven weeks, two of them after their high command had surrendered. 68% casualty rate.

ENSIGN
Of course, Sir, I just didn't –

THE OPERATIVE
There.

His glasses stop scrolling and Mal's military file opens, a picture of Mal in one lens.

THE OPERATIVE
If the feds ever bothered to cross-ref justice files with war records... Yes. Our Mr. Reynolds was a sergeant, 57th Overlanders. Volunteer. Fought at Serenity till the very last. This man is an issue. This man hates us.

ENSIGN
First Mate Zoe Washburn, formerly Corporal Zoe Alleyne, also in the 57th. Career army, looks like.

THE OPERATIVE
She's followed him far... Give me

the crew, registered passengers — Our Captain is a passionate man, no room there for subtlety. He's bound to have some very obvious...

CLOSE ON: THE LENS of his glasses. On it is a slowly moving picture of INARA.

THE OPERATIVE
...weakness...

INT. STORAGE LOCKER - NIGHT

River is still asleep, Mal finishing chaining her wrists. She lies on her side, breathing evenly.

Mal stares at her a moment, then:

INT. DINING ROOM - CONTINUING

He exits to find the whole group waiting for him, sans Wash.

SIMON
May I see her?

MAL
She's still napping just now. And I believe you've got some story-telling to do.

WASH
(entering)
We're out of atmo, plotted for Haven. No one following as of yet.

KAYLEE
Haven? We're gonna see Shepherd Book?

MAL
(nodding)
We got to lay low. And I could fair use some spiritual guidance right about now.
(to Simon)
I am a lost lamb; what in hell happened back there?

WASH
Start with the part where Jayne gets knocked out by a ninety pound girl. 'Cause I don't think that's ever getting old.

ZOE
Do we know if anyone was killed?

MAL
It's likely. I know she meant to kill me 'fore the Doc put her to sleep, which how exactly does that work anyhow?

SIMON
Safeword.
(beat)
The people who helped me break River out — they had intel that River and the other subjects were being embedded with behavioral conditioning. They taught me a safeword, in case... something happened.

KAYLEE
Not sure I get it.

SIMON
A phrase that's encoded in her

brain, that makes her fall asleep. If I speak the words, "Eta —

JAYNE
(jumping back)
Well don't say it!

ZOE
It only works on her, Jayne.

JAYNE
Oh. Well, now I know that.

MAL
"In case something happened."

SIMON
What?

MAL
You feel to elaborate on what that something might be? I mean they taught you that fancy safeword, they must've figured she was gonna, what — start uncontrollably crocheting?

SIMON
They never said what —

MAL
And you never did ask.

Mal grabs him and throws him against the wall, in his face.

MAL
Eight months. Eight months you had her on my boat knowing full

well she might go monkeyshit at the wrong word and you never said a thing —

SIMON
I brought her out here so they couldn't get to her, I don't even know how they —

MAL
My ship. My crew! You had a gorramn timebomb living with us!

INT. STORAGE LOCKER - CONTINUING

River's eyes open.

INT. DINING ROOM - CONTINUING

MAL
What if she went off in the mid-dle of dinner, or in bunk with Kaylee, did that give you a moment's pause?

Simon looks at Kaylee, the truth of Mal's words hitting him.

SIMON
I thought she was getting better.

JAYNE
And I thought they was gettin' off!
(off looks)
Didn't we have a intricate plan how they was gonna be not here anymore?

KAYLEE
We couldn't leave them now...!

JAYNE
No, now that she's a... killer woman
we ought be bringin' 'em tea and
dumplings!
(to Mal)
In earnest, Mal: why'd you bring her
back on?

Mal looks at Jayne, at all of them.
Doesn't have an answer.

SIMON
May I see her.

Mal steps aside. Simon enters
the locker.

JAYNE
She goes woolly again, we're gonna
have to put a bullet to her.

**INT. STORAGE LOCKER -
CONTINUING**

River mouths the next words right
along with Mal:

INT. DINING ROOM - CONTINUING

MAL
It's crossed my mind.

WASH
Can I make a suggestion that
doesn't involve violence, or is this
the wrong crowd?

ZOE
Honey...

WASH
Fanty and Mingo might be coming hard down on us, or the
laws... or maybe nobody could be
bunged about our little social
brawl. We need to get our bearings. I think we need to talk to
Mr. Universe.

EXT. SPACE - VFX - NIGHT

The camera swoops in at a spark-
ing ion cloud, then through the
cloud at a barren, metallic satellite moon. Then further in to
reveal a sprawling — and com-

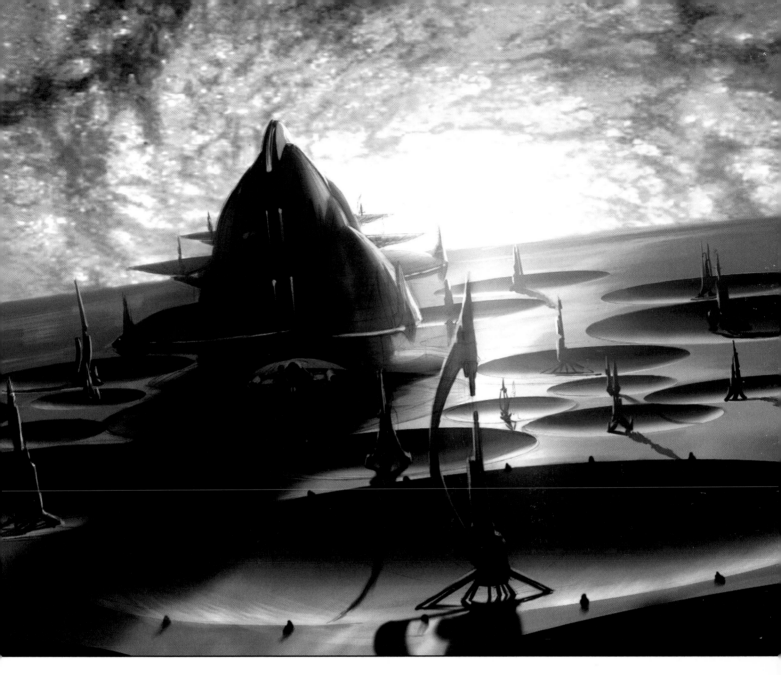

pletely empty — communications complex. Giant satellite dishes everywhere.

INT. MR UNIVERSE'S HQ - CONTINUING

Inside, we find an unkempt young man. Also sleep-deprived, over-caffeinated and kinda sweet. This is MR UNIVERSE. He is alone but for his mannikin-like Love-bot, Lenore.

He's surrounded by screens, computers, feeds — machinery that looks both ultra-modern and long neglected. All the screens play different images — it's a mediaverse.

INT. BRIDGE - CONTINUING

As he watches the security feed of River's fight his image becomes a vidscreen. He's addressing Wash, Mal and Zoe.

We intercut between the two spaces:

MR UNIVERSE
Oh, this is good. This is...
(giggles)
...she's beating up all the burly men and I'm having a catharsis, it's happening right now, you guys always bring me the very best violence. You think you're in a hot place?

WASH
That's what we're looking to learn. Is there any follow up, a newswave...

MR UNIVERSE
There is no "news", there's the truth of the signal, what I see, and there's the puppet theatre the Parliament's jesters foist on the somnambulant public. Monkey taught to say the word "monkey" — lead story on 32 planets. But the slum riots on Hera, not a —

MAL
What about this? Did this make the... puppet theatre?

MR UNIVERSE
No sir. And no lawforce flags, either — I hadda go into the security feed direct...

MAL
You can do that?

MR UNIVERSE
Can't stop the signal, Mal. Everything goes somewhere and I go everywhere. Security feeds are a traipse to access — and I wasn't the first one in, this has prints on it — oh! Look at her go! Everyone is getting bruises and contusions. Contoooosions.

ZOE
(to Mal, over that)
So somebody else has been fed this. That doesn't like me too well.

MR UNIVERSE
Zoe, you sultry minx, stop falling in love with me. You're just gonna embarrass yourself.

As he continues, footage comes up on a monitor behind him: His wedding (in this very space). He steps on the cup, tosses confetti, waves at the camera... Lenore is unmoving — in fact it's not clear whether she DOES move.

MR UNIVERSE
I have a commitment to my Lovebot, it was a very beautiful ceremony, Lenore wrote her own vows, I cried like a baby, a hungry, angry baby.
(re: screen)
And she falls asleep. Which, she would be sleepy.

MAL
Can you go back? See if anybody spoke with her 'fore she acted up, made any kind of contact with her...

Mr Universe works the screen. The image rewinds and stops on River coming up to it, looking at it. She whispers the word, "Miranda", and starts to move away.

MAL
Miranda...? Go back further.

MR UNIVERSE
No...

He pulls another screen close, starts working that one. Matching timecodes, he pulls up the commercial.

MAL
Um... please?

Mr Universe has a third screen showing the commercial as well — and it starts breaking down, bursts of (non-Matrixy) code showing through. As he does so:

MR UNIVERSE
Friends and potential lovers, I have good news and I have the other kind. Good is you're very smart. Someone is talking to her.

WASH
The oaty bar?

MAL
Subliminal. It's a subliminal message broadwaved to trigger her.

MR UNIVERSE
(nodding)
I been seeing this code pop up all over, last few weeks. And I cannot crack it. It's Alliance and it's high military, so here then is the bad. Someone has gone to enormous trouble to find your little friend. And found her they have.

Mal, Zoe and Wash look at each other.

MR UNIVERSE
Do you all know what it is you're carrying?

INT. STORAGE LOCKER - NIGHT

River stares at us, impassive, as the camera pulls away from her to reveal Simon, who is cleaning blood off her face.

RIVER
They're afraid of me.

SIMON
I'm sorry...

RIVER
They should be. What I will show them... Oh God...

She starts tearing up, breathing faster... Simon runs his hands through her hair.

SIMON
It's okay, it's okay...

RIVER
(somewhere else)
Show me off like a dog, old men covered in blood, it never touched them but they're drowning in it... so much loss... I don't know what I'm saying. I never know what I'm saying...

SIMON
In the Maidenhead, you said something. When you were triggered, do you remember? The Captain saw you say something on the feed...

RIVER
Miranda.

Opposite: 'The ramp lowers to reveal Shepherd Book'.

Below: The storage locker scene. Joss Whedon: 'The places Summer goes to and the way Sean stays with her and supports her in that scene I find just heartrending.'

SIMON
Miranda.

RIVER
(laughs bitterly)
Ask her. She'll show you all.

SIMON
Show us what? Who is Miranda?
(beat)
Am I... talking to Miranda now?

She shoots him a look.

RIVER
I'm not a multiple, dumbo.

SIMON
No. Right. But I think somehow when they triggered you it brought this up, this memory

RIVER
It isn't mine. The memory. I didn't bring it and I shouldn't have to carry it, it isn't mine.
(urgently:)

Don't make me sleep again.

SIMON
I won't.

RIVER
Put a bullet to me. Bullet in the brain pan, squish.

SIMON
Don't say that. Not ever. We'll get through this.

She reaches out and touches his face, affectionately.

RIVER
Things are going to get much much worse.

SIMON
Well, the Captain hasn't tossed us in the airlock, so I'd say we're —

RIVER
He has to see. More than anyone... he has to see what he doesn't want to.

SIMON
River. What will Miranda show us.

She thinks.

RIVER
Death.

SIMON
Whose death?

And she starts laughing. Quietly at first, then louder, then almost uncontrollably, screaming in his face:

RIVER
EVERYBODY'S!!!

SMASH CUT TO:

Black Silence.

INT. CAVE - VFX - DAY

It's pitch black here, til Serenity's lights throw a hard relief on the

rocky wall. She flies in after, slow and steady, revealing herself to be in a huge mineshaft.

BOOK (O.S.)
Lord, I am walking your way.

INT. MINE CAVE - DAY

THE RAMP lowers to reveal Shepherd BOOK, a working-class preacher and former crew member. A couple of miners pass behind him. Book smiles as the Serenity crew comes out to meet him:

BOOK (O.S.)
Let me in, for my feet are sore, my clothes are ragged.

EXT. MINING CAMP - DAY

We see the camp: a few shacks and a working mine (and one small patch of ragged vegetable garden), as our group come down to it, greeted by a few miners, including an eight year-old boy that rushes to Kaylee...

ANGLE ON: A CANNON mounted at the edge of town. The guy manning it sees them arrive, also goes to greet them.

**INT. COMMUNITY
KITCHEN - NIGHT**

We see the gang sitting and eating. Comfortable, even laughing a bit. Jayne presents Book with a couple of cigars. Kaylee hoists the boy on her lap.

BOOK (O.S.)
Look in my eyes, Lord, and my sins will play out on them as on a screen. Read them all.

EXT. MINING CAMP - NIGHT

Most of the camp is asleep. Jayne and Kaylee sit with a few miners as Jayne plucks out a tune on something that very closely resembles a guitar.

Mal approaches Book on the edge of a rise overlooking the others. Mal has a bowl and chopsticks. Book is finishing:

BOOK
Forgive what you can, and send me on my path. I will walk on, until you bid me rest.

MAL
Hope that ain't for me, Shepherd.

BOOK
(lighting a cigar)
It's prayer for the dead.

MAL
Then I really hope it ain't for me.

BOOK
It's for the men River might have killed in that bar.

MAL
Weren't River that did it, you know that. Somebody decided her brain was just another piece of property to take, fenced it right up.

BOOK
You got a plan?

MAL
Hiding ain't a plan?

BOOK
It'll do you for a spell, and the folks here'll be glad of the extra coin...

MAL
...but the Alliance'll be coming. They're after this girl with a powerful will. I look to hear the tromp of their boots any moment.

As Book replies, puts out his cigar, saving most of it for another time.

BOOK
You won't.
(off Mal's look)
This isn't a palms-up military run, Mal. No reports broadwaved, no warrants... much as they want her,

they want her hid. That means Closed File. Means an Operative, which is trouble you've not known.

MAL
I coulda left her there.

INT. STORAGE LOCKER - NIGHT

As he continues, we see an image of him watching over the sleeping girl, his mind racing.

RON GLASS

In a certain kind of way, Book sees himself in Mal. At another time, before his conversion, they might have been partners. Because of that, I think that his intention and conviction and desire to have Mal realize the brighter side of himself, is something that really engages me [as an actor]. But Book knows that Mal's the kind of guy that you can't have that kind of confrontation with. So [he has to] inspire, to cajole. You know, so that it happens without a whole lot of push.

Because of the life that Book had before he decided to be a preacher, he has an enormous amount of skill in a lot of different areas. And an enormous amount of knowledge about a lot of different things...

MAL (O.S.)
I had an out — hell, I had every reason in the 'verse to leave her lay and haul anchor.

EXT. MINING CAMP - CONTINUING

BOOK
Not your way, Mal.

MAL
I have a way?
(thinks)
Is that better than a plan?

BOOK
You can play the thug all you want, but there's more to you than you're ever like to 'fess.

MAL
You just think that 'cause my eyes is all sorrowful and pretty.

BOOK
Only one thing is gonna walk you through this, Mal. Belief.

MAL
Sermons make me sleepy, Shepherd. I ain't looking for help from on

high. That's a long wait for a train don't come.

BOOK
When I talk about belief, why do you always assume I'm talking about God?
(Mal has no response)
They'll come at you sideways.

As he continues, we see:

EXT. COMPANION TRAINING HOUSE - DAY

Inara stands waiting, her back to us, in front of the very vista we first saw her before.

The Operative comes slowly up the staircase, stands before her.

BOOK (V.O.)
It's how they think: sideways. It's how they move. Sidle up and smile, hit you where you're weak.

EXT. MINING CAMP - CONTINUING

BOOK
Sorta man they're like to send

believes hard. Kills and never
asks why.

MAL
It's of interest to me how much you
seem to know about that world.

BOOK
I wasn't born a Shepherd, Mal.

MAL
Have to tell me about that some time.

BOOK
(looking out)
No I don't.

He walks away, offering this:

BOOK
Sideways.

Mal watches him go, thinking.

EXT. CLASSROOM - DAY

The Teacher from the very
beginning is standing in front of
River, whose desktop screen depicts
a single, dark planet.

TEACHER
River?

Little River is working away, not
paying attention.

TEACHER
River, you look tired. I think everybody's a little tired by now; why
don't we all lie down.

River looks up, scared. All the other
children wordlessly get up from
their seats and lie on the floor next
to them.

TEACHER
A little peace and quiet will make
everything better.

She starts to lie down herself, right
on the grass.

RIVER
No...

TEACHER
River. Do as you're told. It's going to
be fine. Lie down.

RIVER
NO!

INT. STORAGE LOCKER - NIGHT

River starts awake.

INT. MAL'S ROOM - CONTINUING

Mal does too, shirtless on his
bunk.

MAL
Whuh huh nuhwhat?

WASH (O.S.)
(for the third time)

Mal! You up? Got a wave. I'm a
bounce it down to you.

He pops up, turns to the screen as
the white noise becomes:

MAL
Inara.

INT. INARA'S ROOM

(Coverage for vidphone only.)

BACK IN MAL'S ROOM

REVERSE ON: Inara on Mal's
screen. We see her from about
chest level up. She, presumably,
sees the same.

INARA
Mal. I uh, is this a bad time?

MAL
Good as any.

INARA
Please tell me you're wearing pants.

MAL
(slight grin)
Naked as the day I come cryin'.
How's your world?

INARA
Cold. It's autumn here.

MAL
Still at the Training House?

INARA
Right where you left me.

MAL
I remember it as nice enough.
Picturesque.

INARA
It is that. What about you?

MAL
Still flying. So what occasions the
wave? Not that to see you ain't...
well you look very fine...

INT. BRIDGE - CONTINUING

Zoe and Wash are secretly watching
both Mal and Inara on two different
screens, smiling at their formal
shyness.

Jayne enters, wondering what's up...

INT. MAL'S ROOM - CONTINUING

INARA
Oh. Thank you, I... I guess we
have something of a problem
here. With the locals, I thought
maybe...

MAL
You could use a gun hand?

INARA
I'm hoping not. But if you were
close at all, you — the crew —
could take your ease here a
while... and there'd be payment...

MAL
Payment is never not a factor. I
could sound out the crew... This
pot like to boil over soon?

INARA
Soon. Not right away.

MAL
Well, it would be, I mean I would like to... Kaylee's been missing you something fierce —

INT. BRIDGE - CONTINUING

There is a general groan among the audience, which now includes Kaylee as well...

KAYLEE
Oh they're so pathetic!

INT. MAL'S ROOM - CONTINUING

INARA
I miss her too. I even miss my shuttle, occasionally.

MAL
Yeah, you left a... got some of your stuff in a trunk, never did get a chance to drop it off.

INARA
I didn't mean to leave stuff —

MAL
I didn't look through the... stuff... just sundries I expect.

Now that they're both done lying, Inara smiles blandly, nods. An awkward beat.

MAL
Well, it's kind of late where I'm at. I'll send a wave as soon as I can.

INARA
Thank you.

She disappears. Mal thinks a moment.

INT. BRIDGE - MOMENTS LATER

Mal comes up in, buttoning his shirt.

WASH
Inara. Nice to see her again.

ZOE
So, trap?

MAL
Trap.

ZOE
We goin' in?

MAL
It ain't but a few hours out...

WASH
Yeah, but, remember the part where it's a trap?

MAL
If that's the case, then Inara's already caught in it. She wouldn't set us up willing. Might be we got a shot at seeing who's turning these wheels. We go in.

KAYLEE
How can you be sure Inara don't just wanna see you? Sometimes peo-

ple have feelings — I'm referring here to people...

MAL
Y'all were watching, I take it.

Guilty glances.

KAYLEE
Yes.

MAL
You see us fight?

KAYLEE
No.

MAL
Trap.

EXT. SERENITY - DAY

The ship moves gracefully over the mountains.

INT. BRIDGE - CONTINUING

WASH
We're about seventy miles from the Training house. And nobody on radar... if the Alliance is about, they're laying low.

MAL
They're about. Find us a home. I'll take the shuttle in closer. Zoe, ship is yours.

He starts out, turns back to Zoe.

Above: The set for Inara's
'sparsely lush' room,
complete with a statue of
Buddha.

Opposite: 'I can be very
graceful when I need to.'

MAL
Remember: if anything happens to
me, or you don't hear from me within the hour... you take this ship and
you come and rescue me.

ZOE
What? And risk my ship?

MAL
(exiting)
I mean it. It's cold out there. I don't
wanna get left.

EXT. SERENITY - DAY

She is nestled in a gorge, overhang-
ing rocks all but burying her from
view. The shuttle on the right lifts
off from the side of the ship and
glides off, keeping low.

**EXT. COMPANION TRAINING
HOUSE - DAY**

A line of young trainees files by in
robes and red shawls pulled over
their heads — one trainee a good
deal larger than the others.

INT. INARA'S ROOM - LATER

She is kneeling in front of a statue of Buddha, lighting a few
incense sticks.

The room is sparsely lush — not
as opulent as the shuttle where
she entertained men, but still
beautifully furnished and draped.
A lace curtain hangs in front of
the light, casting its pattern in
shadow over everything.

Including the rather large figure
in a red shawl who kneels beside
Inara.

MAL
Dear Buddha, please send me a
pony, and a plastic rocket, and —

INARA
Mal! What are you doing here?

MAL
You invited me.

INARA
I never thought for a second
you'd be stupid enough to come!

MAL
Well that makes you kind of a
tease, doesn't it?

I have to say, I'm impressed that you would come for her yourself. And that you would make it this far in that outfit.

MAL
(standing)
I can be very graceful when I need to.

THE OPERATIVE
I've no doubt.

Mal sheds his shawl and robe. Inara kneels at the altar, picks out another incense stick.

MAL
What are you doing?

INARA
I'm praying for you, Mal.

THE OPERATIVE
That's very thoughtful. But I mean it when I say you're not in any danger.

MAL
Speak your piece.

THE OPERATIVE
I think you're beginning to under-

stand how dangerous River Tam is.

MAL
She is a mite unpredictable. Mood swings, of a sort.

THE OPERATIVE
It's worse than you know.

MAL
It usually is.

THE OPERATIVE
That girl will rain destruction down on you and your ship. She's an albatross, Captain.

MAL
Way I remember it, albatross was a ship's good luck... til some idiot killed it.
(to Inara)
Yes, I've read a poem. Try not to faint.

The Operative moves further into the room. Whenever he moves, Mal counters.

THE OPERATIVE
I've seen your war record. I know how you must feel about the Alliance.

INARA
You knew my invitation wasn't on the level —

MAL
Which led me to the conclusion that you must be in some trouble.

INARA
I'm fine! I'm... giddy.

MAL
For a woman schooled in telling men what they wanna hear, you ain't much of a liar.

INARA
Mal, you cannot handle this man.

THE OPERATIVE
(entering)

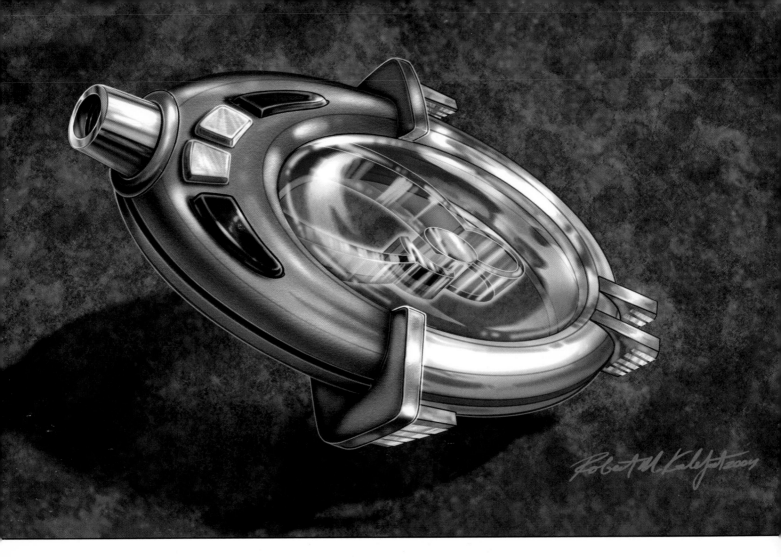

MAL
You really don't.

THE OPERATIVE
Fair to say. But I have to hope you understand you can't beat us.

MAL
I got no need to beat you. I just wanna go my way.

THE OPERATIVE
And you can do that, once you let me take River Tam back home.

MAL
No, no, you're working this deal all crabbed. You got to open with pay-ment. Make a flush offer and then we'll see where this conversation goes.

THE OPERATIVE
(shaking his head)
That's a trap. I offer money you'll play the man of honor and take umbrage. I ask you to do what's

right, you'll play the brigand. I've no stomach for games; I already know you'll not see reason.

MAL
Alliance wanted to show me reason, they shouldn't have sent an assassin.

The Operative is stopped by this. Unhappily, he continues:

THE OPERATIVE
I have a warship in deep orbit, Captain. We locked on to Serenity's pulse beacon the moment you hit atmo. I can speak a word and send a missile to that exact location inside of three minutes.

Mal pulls a small device, clipped wires sticking out all around it, and tosses it to the Operative.

MAL
You do that, best make peace with your dear and fluffy lord.

THE OPERATIVE
Pulse beacon.

MAL
Advice from an old tracker: you wanna find someone, use your eyes.

THE OPERATIVE
How long do you think you can really run from us?

MAL
Oh, a jack-rabbit, me. 'Sides, I never credited the Alliance with an over-abundance of brains. And if you're the best they got...

THE OPERATIVE
Captain Reynolds, I should tell you so that you don't waste your time: You can't make me angry.

INARA
Oh please. Spend an hour with him.

Mal smiles — then glares at Inara, mouthing "Hey!"

THE OPERATIVE
I need her, Captain. River is... my purpose and I will gather her to me. The brother as well. Whatever else happens is incidental. In the greater scheme.

MAL
Why is it that the greater scheme always makes everything not that great?

THE OPERATIVE
I want to resolve this like civilized men. I'm not threatening you. I'm unarmed.

MAL
Good!

He draws and shoots the Operative in the chest. The Operative goes down as Mal grabs Inara, moves for the doorway.

The Operative is on him in a second, choke-hold from behind.

THE OPERATIVE
I am of course wearing full body armor. I'm not a moron.

He tosses Mal hard against a wall, spinning and blocking a blow from Inara — she is clearly trained in martial arts, but he flat-heels her to the ground within seconds.

Mal is going for his gun again, turning, and the Operative kicks him in the face, sends him back, gun flying. Mal gets to his feet and they square off. Mal breathing hard, nose dripping blood. The Operative perfectly poised, waiting.

MAL
No back up? We're making an awful ruckus...

THE OPERATIVE
They'll come when they're needed.

MAL
I'd start whistling.

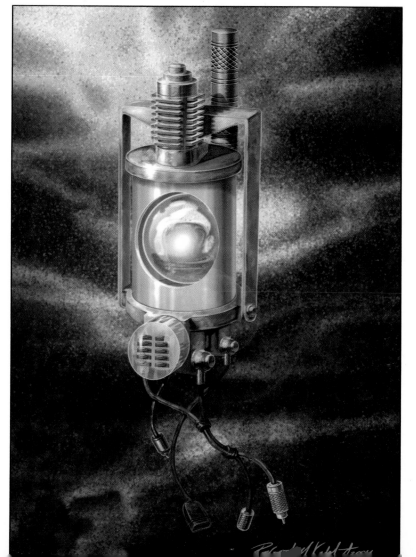

THE OPERATIVE
Captain, what do you think is going to happen here?

They come at each other. The Operative is the much better trained — he's fluid, his blows sparse and deadly. Mal is more bluster and determination, and the Operative's precision is wearing Mal down.

Mal punches wild — the Operative counters with a spin-kick to the head that sends Mal to the ground not far from Inara, breathing hard. He tries to rise again, painfully, but Inara places her hand on his arm.

The Operative goes to his briefcase by the door, pulls out his sword. His face has taken on that remote kind of fascination as he looks at it.

THE OPERATIVE
Nothing here is what it seems.

INARA
I know.

THE OPERATIVE
He's not the plucky hero. The Alliance isn't some evil empire. This isn't the grand arena.

INARA
And that's not incense.

He turns to look: the incense stick burns away — rather like a fuse — and FLASHES in an explosion of light and sound.

COSTUME DESIGN:
INARA

Costume designer Ruth E. Carter: 'Inara is a glamorous character. [For the movie] we are trying to amp her look up — what more could we do? And yet we wanted to be different. So we tried hundreds of things on her, [combining] a Western look with an Eastern look with another — we would take an obi and wrap it around a sari and create a look that wasn't saying one particular thing.'

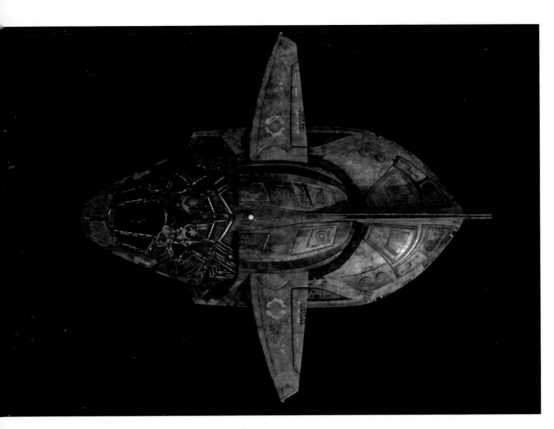

It's a flash-bomb: The Operative sails back as everything goes smoky white and the sound dies to a tiny buzz.

The Operative tries to get his bearings — and four armored soldiers are in his face, asking him for orders... Mal and Inara are gone. He motions for the men to follow them.

THE OPERATIVE
Just a flash bomb. Go! Go!

INT. COMPANION TRAINING HOUSE - CONTINUING

Inara leads Mal (who is reholstering his gun) down some steps and along a corridor. The sound is still tinny and weird.

MAL
...I had him...

INARA
What?

MAL
(deafly loud)
I think that I was winning!

They come down the shallow stone stairs — she presses a hidden lever and one stone landing slides under the stair above, revealing a trapdoor. They start down it.

EXT. SIDE OF MOUNTAIN, BY MAL'S SHUTTLE - DAY

Mal and Inara move quickly down the mountain. They look to see that Mal's shuttle has three Alliance guards waiting by it. Mal ducks back out of sight, pulls a fancy-looking grenade out of his pocket. Pops the top and hurls it over at the foursome.

CLOSE ON: THE GRENADE, as a series of bars of light go out one by one, counting down —

ALLIANCE SOLDIER
Grenade!

Everybody dives for cover. The moment they do, Mal and Inara race into the shuttle, Mal sweeping up the grenade just as the last light goes out and nothing happens.

One soldier turns to look and Mal shoots him back down as the door shuts on him and Inara.

INT. SHUTTLE - CONTINUING

Inara pushes into the pilot's seat.

INARA
Hang on to something.

MAL
You sure you remember how it —

He nearly falls over as:

EXT. MOUNTAIN RANGE - CONTINUING

The shuttle shoots straight up, spinning and heading out.

INT. SHUTTLE - CONTINUING

Inara stares straight ahead, relaxing her grip on the controls. Mal is gone.

INARA
I told you to hang on.

MAL (O.S.)
(in great pain)
I'm fine...

EXT. SPACE - VFX - LATER

We are below Serenity as her bay doors are closing, six little objects floating out of her belly like roe. These objects are roughly the size of pony-kegs, and clearly homemade, parts welded together almost haphazardly. They all spark silently to life — and shoot off in six different directions, as Serenity herself fires up her Firefly effect and burns away from us.

EXT. COMPANION TRAINING HOUSE - DAY

The Operative sips tea and rubs his temple.

THE OPERATIVE
(into a com)
Forget the pulse beacon, there has to be another way to track the ship — get a read on the nav sat. It's a

registered transport, you must be able to locate —

ENSIGN (O.S.)
Sir?

THE OPERATIVE
Have you found a nav sat trajectory?

ENSIGN (O.S.)
Sir... we've found seven.

The Operative looks more unhappy than angry.

THE OPERATIVE
(to himself)
Does he think this is a game?

EXT. CLASSROOM - DAY

The teacher and students sleep as River — as we saw her in the institute, older, with blood seeping from the needle-holes in her head — makes her way through them.

Slowly she looks down at her desk. On it is the solar system, glowing lines connecting all the stars and planets. She becomes

wide-eyed, breathing hard as it pushes in to one system, one planet...

She looks over to one side of the tent, and we see:

INT. LAB - CONTINUING

Her POV is of the lab. There stand some five older men in formal dress. They stare at her, impassive.

INT./EXT. FLASHBACKS

We see flashes of corpses, lying in houses, in city streets—

EXT. CLASSROOM - DAY

River gets more and more agitated — and a REAVER is next to her in frame, grabbing her throat, bearing his sharpened teeth to bite off her face —

INT. STORAGE LOCKER - DAY

And River awakens. A moment to get her bearings, then her eyes narrow with intent.

INARA (V.O.)
We have every reason to be afraid.

INT. PASSENGER DORM - CONTINUING

JAYNE
Why, 'cause this guy beat up Mal? That ain't so hard —

MAL
He didn't beat me up —

INARA
Because he's a believer.

INT. THE OPERATIVE'S SHIP, A DARK CABIN

As Inara continues, we see: Fanty and Mingo, tied to chairs. Light spills onto their bruised faces as the Operative enters.

INARA (V.O.)
He's intelligent, methodical and devout in his belief that killing River is the right thing to do.

INT. PASSENGER DORM - CONTINUING

Above and opposite: An example of computer-aided set design. 3D mock-ups of some of the Serenity interiors.

INARA
I honestly think the only reason we haven't been blown out of the air is that he needs to see her.

SIMON
Needs to see her why?

INARA
I'm uncertain. I would say to be sure of the kill, but... I just know he'll kill us all to get to her.

JAYNE
So no hope of a reward, huh?

ZOE
Did he mention a deal of any kind?

MAL
(looking at Simon)
Give the two of them up. Go my way.

JAYNE
Which you was all ready to do not a day ago. What went sour?

MAL
Cutting them loose ain't the same as handing them over.

JAYNE
That so? 'Cause the corpse I'm about to become is having trouble telling the difference.

SIMON
(to Inara)
Did he say anything about a "Miranda"?

INARA
What is that?

ZOE
Don't know who or what, but it's on River's mind.

MAL
Conjure it might be the reason he's after her.

INARA
You think maybe it poses some kind of threat to the Alliance?

WASH
Do we care? Are we caring about that?

JAYNE
You dumbass hogs, the only people she's a threat to is us on this boat!

INT. STORAGE LOCKER - CONTINUING

River is near the ceiling, keeping herself up in a split again, feet against the walls. There is a wire mesh cover to the light, and she has bent part of it out, is working it inside the lock of her shackles.

INT. PASSENGER DORM - MOMENTS LATER

The argument continues. We are on Mal, who is trying to hide his increasing agitation.

JAYNE (O.C.)
We take a shuttle, we drop her off and we get 'em off our backs —

ZOE (O.C.)
(over "get 'em off")
You think it stops there? What if they keep coming —

JAYNE (O.C.)
(also interrupting)
And what if she pops again?

Whip off Mal to Inara:

INARA
(to Mal)
You can't keep her in the storage locker forever, Mal. What are you gonna do when —

MAL
I don't know.

INARA
"I don't know" is not a good answer.

MAL
(starting to cross)

Look, we get back to Haven in a few hours' time....

JAYNE
Hiding under the Shepherd's skirts, that's a manful scheme —

MAL
You wanna run this ship?

JAYNE
Yes!

MAL
(small beat)
Well you can't!

JAYNE
Do a damn sight better job'n you. Getting us lashed over a couple of strays...
(to Simon)
No offense, Doc, I think it's noble as a grape the way you look to River, but she ain't my sister
(to Mal)
and she ain't your crew. Oh, and neither is she exactly helpless! So where's it writ we gotta lay down our lives for her, which is what you've steered us toward.

MAL
I didn't start this.

JAYNE
No, the Alliance starts the war — and then you volunteer. Battle of Serenity, Mal: besides Zoe here, how many —
(Mal turns away)
— I'm talkin' at you — how many men in your platoon came out of there alive?

Mal stares at him.

ZOE
(dead cold)
You wanna leave this room.

JAYNE
You're damn right I do.

He stalks upstairs. There's a quiet moment.

INARA
This isn't the war, Mal.

Mal turns, eyeing her.

MAL
Are you telling me that because you think I don't know —

INARA
You came to the training house looking for a fight.

MAL
I came looking for you.

INARA
I just want to know who I'm dealing with. I've seen too many versions of you to be sure.

MAL
I start fighting a war I guarantee you'll see something new.

Mal walks out into the cargo bay, Inara following, over:

SIMON
We'll get off. River and I'll get off at Haven and find some —

KAYLEE
Nobody's saying that.

WASH
Nobody besides Jayne is saying that.

INT. CARGO BAY - CONTINUING

Inara tries to catch up to —

INARA
Mal.

MAL
(turning)

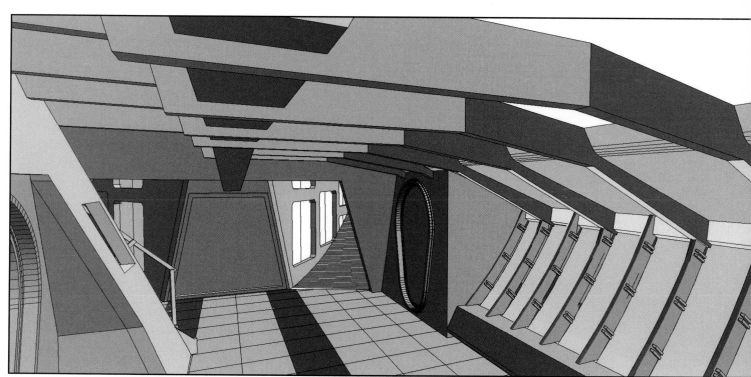

I got no answers for you, Inara. I got no rudder. Wind blows northerly, I go north. That's who I am. Maybe that ain't a man to lead but they have to follow so you wanna tear me down do it inside your own mind.

INARA
I'm not trying to tear you down —

MAL
But you fog things up. You always have — you spin me about. I wish like hell you was elsewhere.

INARA
I was.

INT. DINING ROOM - CONTINUING

Jayne is looking at the storage locker door. A beat.

JAYNE
(Chinese)
Go HWONG-TONG.
[English: Enough of this nonsense.]

He moves to the aft hall, shuts and locks the door. Goes back to the locker and starts to unlock it, pulling his gun.

JAYNE
No trouble now, little crazy person... we're going for a nice shuttle ride —

He opens the door and she is on him in an instant, whip blow to the throat, the nose — he fires wildly as she jumps on him, wraps her arms around his neck and topples him back —

INT. AFT HALL - MOMENTS LATER

The crew enters, drawn by the shots. Mal is first — can't open the door. Looks in to see an unconscious Jayne...

MAL
The other way! Find her and do not engage!

Everyone piles out the other way. Simon remains, to look in the window.

ANGLE: SIMON'S POV: There is Jayne, not moving — and River pops up right in front of us.
He starts, then waits as she opens the door.

SIMON
It's gonna be oka —

She elbows his throat viciously. He drops to his knees, shocked and gasping, as she spin-kicks him to the ground. He doesn't move. She looks at him a moment, then takes off.

INT. CARGO BAY - MOMENTS LATER

Mal is throwing his shoulder against the bolted door to the upstairs. He gives up, looking around.

ZOE
She's sealed off the bridge. I do not like her there.

KAYLEE
Cap'n!

She tosses him a bolt remover. He starts pulling a bolt out of a panel on the wall, tells Zoe:

MAL
Check the shuttles. She coulda snuck in.

He pops the panel off and starts wriggling in among the wires.

INT. FOREDECK HALL/ BRIDGE - LATER

A floor panel hinges open, Mal pulling himself up. He moves quietly to the bridge, gun drawn.

He enters to find River frantically punching up coordinates on a big Cortex screen she's pulled out by the copilot's seat. She whips Jayne's gun at his face, never looking at him. A moment, and Mal lowers his own gun.

MAL
The government's man, he says you're a danger to us. Not worth helping. Is he right? Are you anything but a weapon? I've staked my crew's life on the theory that you're a person, actual and whole, and if I'm wrong you'd best shoot me now.
(she cocks the gun)
Or we could talk more...

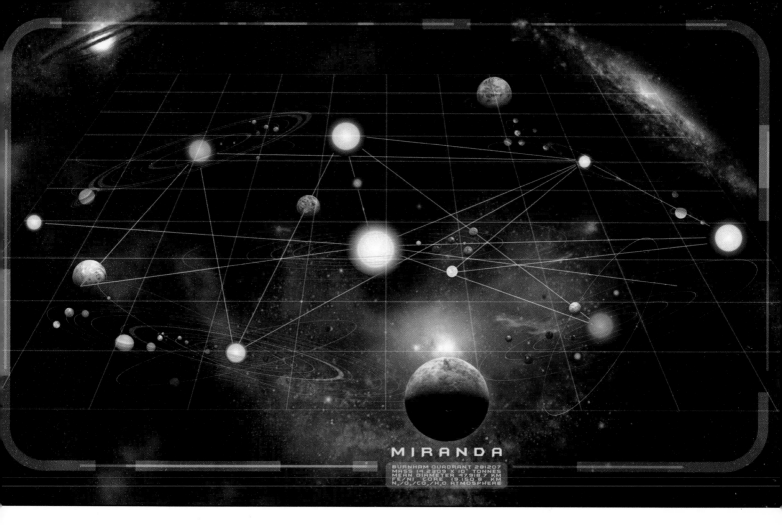

MIRANDA

BURNHAM QUADRANT 281207
MASS 14.2309 X 10⁷ TONNES
MEAN DIAMETER 4791.8 7 KM
FE/NI CORE 19.150 8 KM
N₂/O₂/CO₂/H₂O ATMOSPHERE

RIVER
(pointing to screen)
Miranda.

It's a planet. Matches the one from her dream.

INT. BRIDGE - LATER

Everyone has gathered. Wash is piloting now, as they are in atmosphere. River is by Simon. She moves restlessly, upset.

KAYLEE
How can it be there's a whole planet called Miranda and none of us knowed that?

MAL
Because there isn't one. It's a black-rock. Uninhabitable. Terraforming didn't hold, or somesuch. Few settlers died.

RIVER
(to Simon)
I had to show them. I didn't know if you were going to make me sleep.

SIMON
(hoarse whisper)
You could've asked...

KAYLEE
(re: planet)
Wait a tick, yeah! Some years back, before the war. There was call for workers to settle on Miranda, my daddy talked about going. I should've recalled...

WASH
But there's nothing about it on the Cortex — History, Astronomy... it's not in there.

MAL
Half of writing history is hiding the truth. There's something on this rock the Alliance doesn't want known.

INARA
That's right at the edge of the Burnham Quadrant, right? Furthest planet out.
(Mal nods)
It's not that far from here...

WASH
Whoa, no, no —

ZOE
(moving to the screen)
That's a bad notion —

WASH
Honey...

ZOE
I got it, baby.

WASH
Show them the bad...

She hits some commands on the screen, pulls back to reveal a couple of other planets near Miranda.

ZOE
This is us, see? And here's Miranda. All along here, this dead space in between, that's Reaver territory.

WASH
They just float out there, sending out raiding parties —

Above: A map showing the location of the hidden planet, as seen on Serenity's screen.

A lot of who Wash is, is who Zoe is. I draw a lot of who the character is from that. He's a very loving husband, and she's just an intense lady. She's a killer. "[Wash is] just fly the ship, but let's make some money, we'll be great, but once we get some money, let's go on a vacation!" He's that type of guy. He doesn't get too uptight about things, except when people start talkin' about killing. "Why do we got to kill? Let's not do so much killing, please. Everybody just relax." He's that voice on the ship. My wife Zoe does all the fighting. And it's gotta be hard, you know, she goes off to battle, and she might not come back. She's out with the guns and the fighting. And I'm always sittin' on the ship... I'm the getaway driver. But it's fun. He's also a great pilot, you know. That's something that Joss has always said — whenever you need some great flying, Wash is completely calm. That's when he is the most focused, he's not a silly, jokey kind of guy at that point. Everything kinda comes into focus and he can get the job done. Which is cool, because it's nice to play somebody who does their job well.

Opposite: 'I don't care what you believe! Just... believe it. Whatever you have to...'

ZOE
Maybe a hundred ships. And more every year. You go through that you're signing up to be a banquet.

WASH
I'm on board with the run and hide scenario — and we are just about...

He looks at his monitors, looks ahead...

WASH
Wait...

EXT. MINING CAMP - DAY

The ship swings around a mountain to come into view of the camp.

It is a world of fire.

Every building burns, some blown right apart. Bodies litter the scene, not one of them moving. There's a grounded Alliance ship not far from the cannon that shot it down.

INT. BRIDGE - CONTINUING

We see Mal's face as the sight hits him like a gut-punch.

EXT. MINING CAMP - MOMENTS LATER

The crew pours out even as the ramp lowers, going off in all directions, calling out to people. Jayne checks the perimeter, River moves slowly, staring at objects, at details. Kaylee heads for the burning church.

KAYLEE
Shepherd? Shepherd Book!

She stops, looking at the ground by the steeple. There is the body on the ground, face down. The child she played with at dinner. Kaylee stares, at first uncomprehending.

ANGLE: MAL, moving in the other direction, approaches the cannon, Jayne behind him. He stops and sees:

Book, lying by the cannon, torn up badly from the waist down.

MAL
(to Jayne)
Get the Doc.

He moves to the Shepherd, grabs his searching hand.

MAL
Shepherd... Don't move.

BOOK
Won't go far...

MAL
Shouldn't've been you. I'm so sorry, it was... they should've hit us. They should've hit me.

BOOK
That crossed my mind.
(coughs)
I shot him down —

MAL
I seen.

BOOK
I killed the ship... that killed us. Not... very Christian of me.

MAL
You did what's right.

BOOK
(not unkindly)
Coming from you, that means... almost nothing... HNAAH! Ah, I'm long gone...

MAL
Doc'll bring you round. I look to be bored by many more sermons 'fore you slip — don't move —

BOOK
Can't... order me around, boy. I'm not one of your crew.

MAL
Yes you are.

Book coughs up blood, grabbing Mal. Urgent, almost angry.

BOOK
You... it's on you now... all this death, this shit... you have to find a course. This can't mean nothing. River... you have to...

MAL
Come on, keep it up —

Book grabs Mal's face, talks as though replying to something:

BOOK
I don't care what you believe! Just... believe it. Whatever you have to...

His breathing becomes laboured. Hitched.

Stopped. His hand slips away, his blood leaving a distinct print on Mal's face.

Jayne and Simon run up, Simon slowing down — going to the Shepherd, but entirely aware he's dead. Zoe and Wash join them as Jayne looks around him, Mal still fixed on Book.

JAYNE
How come they ain't waiting? They know'd we was coming, how come they only sent one?

Zoe realizes:

ZOE
They didn't know we'd come here...

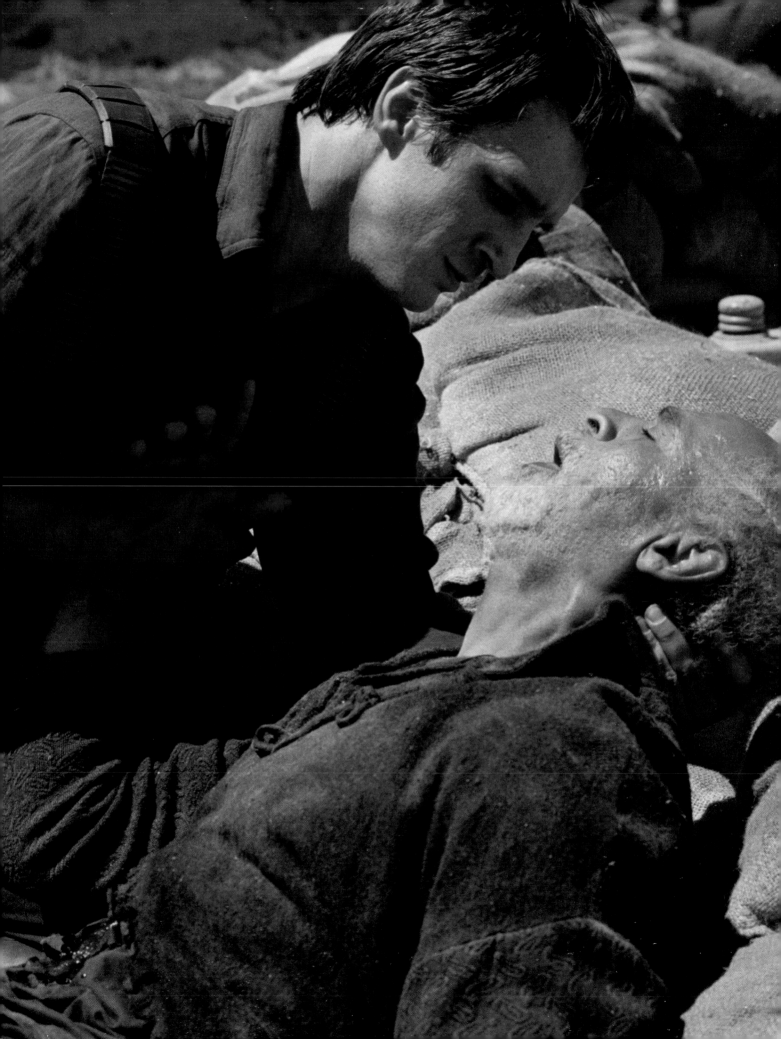

She turns to Wash.

ZOE
Get on the Cortex. Wave the
Sanchez brothers, Li Shen — anyone whose ever sheltered us after a
heist. Tell them to get out. Get
out now.

SMASH CUT TO:

INT. BRIDGE - LATER

Silence.

Every Cortex screen is on, each
looking at a different place. Every
one shows fire, destruction or the
snow of an interrupted signal.

Mal stands alone amidst the
screens, saying nothing. After a
long moment, all of the screens
hitch, the images replaced by
identical images of the Operative.
He looks solemn.

THE OPERATIVE
I'm sorry.

MAL
(uncomprehending)
You — what?

THE OPERATIVE
If your quarry goes to ground,
leave no ground to go to. You
should have taken my offer — or
did you think none of this was
your fault?

MAL
I don't murder childern.

THE OPERATIVE
And as you can see, I do. If I
have to.

MAL
Why? Do you even know why they
sent you?

THE OPERATIVE
It's not my place to ask. I believe
in something that is greater than
myself. A better world. A world
without sin.

MAL
So me and mine got to lie down
and die so you can live in your
better world?

THE OPERATIVE
I'm not going to live there. How
could you think — there's no
place for me there, any more than

there is for you. Malcolm, I'm a
monster. What I do is evil, I've no
illusions about that. But it must
be done.

MAL
Keep on talking. You're not getting a
location trace off this wave.

THE OPERATIVE
And every minute you keep River
Tam from me more people will die.

MAL
You think I care?

THE OPERATIVE
Of course you do. You're not a
Reaver, Mal. You're a human man
and you will never —

Mal flicks a switch and every screen
goes dark.

**EXT. MINING CAMP - MOMENTS
LATER**

Mal comes striding out, where the
crew have been gathering bodies,
laying blankets over them.

MAL
Get these bodies together.

ZOE
We got time for gravedigging?

MAL
Zoe, you and Simon are gonna rope 'em together. Five or six of 'em. I want them laid out on the nose of our ship.

SIMON
Are you insane?

KAYLEE
What do you mean, the bodies...

MAL
Kaylee, I need you to muck the reactor core, just enough to leave a trail and make it read like we're flying without containment, not enough to fry us.

KAYLEE
These people are our friends —

MAL
Kaylee, you got a day's work to do and two hours to do it.
(turns from her)
Jayne, you and Wash hoist up that cannon mount. Goes right on top. Piece or two of the other ship,

stick it on. Any place you can tear hull without inner breach, do that too.
(looking around)
And we're gonna need paint. We're gonna need red paint.

INARA
(Chinese)
RUNtse de FWOtzoo, ching baoYO wuomun...
[English: Oh merciful Buddha protect us...]

ZOE
Sir. Do you really mean to turn our home into an abomination so we can make a suicidal attempt at passing through Reaver space?

MAL
I mean to live. I mean for us to live. The Alliance won't have that, so we go where they won't follow.

JAYNE
God's balls, there's no way we're going out there!

And everybody (save River) is talking at once:

SIMON
What's the point of living if you sink to the level of a savage —

WASH
(Chinese)
Juhguh JEE HUA jun kuhPAH!
[English: There's nothing about this plan that isn't horrific!]

INARA
Please, we should talk this over —

JAYNE
I ain't takin' orders from a man has lost his brainstem —

And in the middle of it, Mal pulls his gun. Jayne, the most in his face, steps back, hand on his.

MAL
This is how it works. Anybody doesn't wanna fly with me anymore, this is your port of harbour. There's a lot of fine ways to die. I'm not waiting for the Alliance to choose mine.

He walks through the group, toward the smashed cockpit of the Alliance fighter. Struggling to get out is the badly wounded

Above: Concept art of the downed Alliance ship.

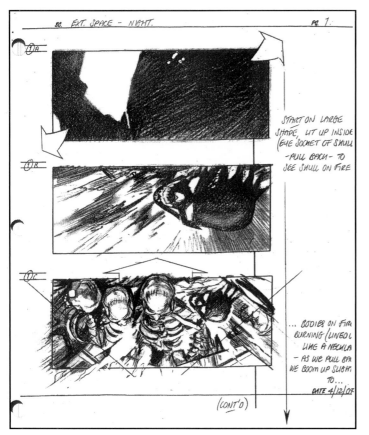

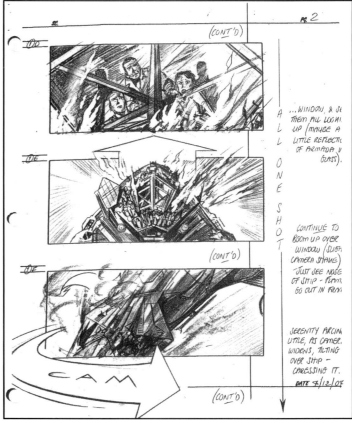

pilot. He sees Mal coming and raises
his hands in surrender.
Mal shoots him in the head, turns
back.

MAL
I mean to confound those bungers,
and take my shot at getting to
Miranda, maybe finding out what all
I'm dying for. That's the only path I
see left and I got to walk it. So I hear
a word out of any of you that ain't
helping me out or taking your leave
I will fucking shoot you.

He grabs a body — drops it at Zoe's
feet as he heads toward the ship.

MAL
Get to work.

He passes River, and we hold on
her, watching him.

**EXT. SPACE/SERENITY BRIDGE -
NIGHT**

CLOSE ON THE BODIES as they
BURN, flames passing over them
and suddenly flickering out as

dark falls. They are patches of
leathered flesh stretched over
bone — monsters, screaming
soundlessly in the nothing of
space.

We arm past them to the windows
of the bridge, looking in at Mal,
watching, with Zoe behind and
Wash at the helm.

And we pull back out to see the
whole of Serenity for the first
time: It is hardly recognizable.
Charred corpses on the nose,
Cannon atop with a space-suited
corpse draped within, long scars,
welded-on parts and war paint...
the trail of green light burns out
with sporadic bursts of vapor.
It looks, for all the world, like a
Reaver ship.

INT. CARGO BAY - CONTINUING

Mal comes down the stairs to the
catwalk. He hesitates, then steps
into the shuttle.

INT. SHUTTLE - CONTINUING

It's dark in here. Mal stands with
his back to the door, no light on
his face, shaking. Not crying, but
overcome.

INARA
Mal.

He looks up: she's in the corner
looking through that trunk of
hers, hands on a long oilcloth
wrapped around something.

MAL
Didn't see you.

INARA
I figured that.

MAL
Anything of use in there?

INARA
Maybe.

She puts it down and crosses to
the bed. He sits by her.

MAL
You don't have to stay in the

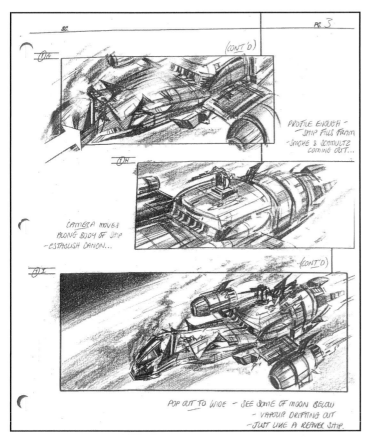

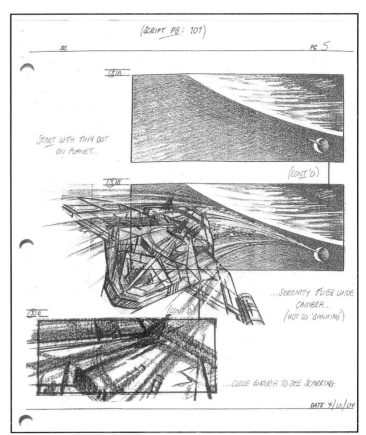

SC.   PG. 3

(CONT'D)

PROFILE ENOUGH –
– SHIP FILLS FRAM
– SMOKE & SCHMULTZ
  COMING OUT...

CAMERA MOVES
ALONG BODY OF SHIP
– ESTABLISH CANON...

(CONT'D)

POP OUT TO WIDE – SEE SOME OF MOON BELOW
– VAPOUR DRIFTING OUT
– JUST LIKE A REAVER SHIP.

(SCRIPT PG: 101)

SC.   PG. 5

START WITH TINY DOT
ON PLANET...

(CONT'D)

...SERENITY FLIES UNDE
CAMERA...
(NOT SO 'BANKING')

(CONT'D)

...CLOSE ENOUGH TO SEE SCARRING.

DATE 8/12/04

shuttle, you know. There's empty rooms, if you wanna sleep awhile.

INARA
You think anyone's set to sleep? Simon's portioning out overdoses of morphine, just in case.

MAL
Cheerful fellow.
(looking around)
Did you really miss this place?

INARA
(rueful smile)
Sometimes... Not so much right now.

A beat. He doesn't look at her when he asks:

MAL
Why did you leave?

She does look at him.

INARA
Why didn't you ask me not to?

Dissatisfied, Mal rises.

MAL
I, uh, I'd better go check on the crew. See how the inevitable mutiny is coming along.

They both want to say more. They don't. He goes.

EXT. SPACE - VFX - NIGHT

Serenity flies, silent.

INT. FOREDECK HALL/BRIDGE - NIGHT

The group make their way toward the bridge. Those close enough to get a view out the window are looking freaked — those already on the bridge are stock still.

Pressed up against the glass of the window is River, just staring.

EXT. SPACE - VFX - CONTINUING

Reverse to see: an armada.

The black sky is filled with what must be ninety ships in a vague cluster, as Serenity breaks frame headed toward them. Most of them hang still in the air. Some move swimmingly about. Some turn in gentle drifts, as though looking around.

INT. BRIDGE - CONTINUING

They all wait, tensed up, as they approach the armada...

EXT. SPACE - VFX - CONTINUING

And arrive, moving slowly through the ranks of ships.

WIL MADOC REES '04

Serenity passes a large, bizarrely shaped ship. It turns, as though watching her. But lets her pass.

Another minute, and Serenity is through the Armada, headed for the small planet just beyond.

INT. THE OPERATIVE'S SHIP - BRIDGE - LATER

The Operative stares blankly at the Ensign.

THE OPERATIVE
Define "disappeared".

The Ensign just looks uncomfortable.

INT. SERENITY: BRIDGE - LATER

Kaylee, Simon and River have left the bridge. The clouds fog the windows, so nothing below is visible.

ZOE
Every reading I'm getting says normal. Oceans, land masses... no tectonic instability or radiation.

WASH
Yeah, but no power, either.

MAL
Nothing at all?

WASH
Wait. Something. Might be a beacon, but it's awful weak.

MAL
Find it.

EXT. SERENITY/MIRANDA - DAY

As she touches down, filling the frame. After a moment Mal, Zoe and Jayne emerge from the airlock in full suits, armed. Zoe reads a handheld scanner...

MAL
Gravity's Earthnorm.

ZOE
O2 levels check, pressure... if there's anything wrong the scanner isn't reading it.

Mal pulls off his helmet. Breathes, looking around him.

MAL
Well something sure as hell ain't right...

WIDER ANGLE: They're in a CITY. Gleaming metal, spread out for miles in every direction. Portions decimated by fires long since cold, others overgrown with weeds, but mostly intact. But silent, as if trapped in amber.

JAYNE
This ain't no little settlement.

Above: Pre-production visualization of Serenity coming into land on Miranda.

ZOE
We flew over at least a dozen cities just as big. Why didn't we hear about this?

MAL
Beacon's up ahead.

EXT. CITY - DAY

Out of their suits now, Mal, Zoe and Jayne take point as the entire crew walks along the street, looking about them. They enter a dark tunnel and motion detectors throw on cold lights.

ZOE
Ho.

She moves rapidly, gun out, to:

ANGLE: A SKELETON
Face-down on the ground, clothes tattered. She examines it as Mal approaches, waving the others back.

ZOE
No entry wound, fractures...

MAL
Poison?

They look at each other... then move on, the group following up some stairs off the road...

ANGLE: the group, from high above, as they make their way through the sterile scape.

Mal steps under a block of some kind — another motion detector starts a commercial banner running sputteringly over his head — it quickly dies.

Jayne approaches a downed hovercraft...

JAYNE
Got another one!

Inside are two skeletons: a grown-up and a small child. Clothes in better condition, and again no sign of violence.

JAYNE
They's just sittin' here. Didn't crash...

ANGLE: RIVER is quietly becoming more and more upset.

CLOSE ON: KAYLEE walks in front of an office building, staying away from the cars as she hears:

JAYNE (O.S.)
Couple more here...

Kaylee takes another step — and the corpse of a man is pressed up against the glass wall right behind her. Mouth open, skin dead blue, terribly skinny... a thing to haunt.

SIMON
(seeing it)
Kaylee... Come this way. Come here. Don't —

But she looks —

KAYLEE
GAAAAaaoh God —

— and steps back, horrified, as the others approach.
It's an office. About half the

employees are there, in chairs or on the ground, all in the same state as the first fellow. We see ANGLES of the corpses as the gang evaluates...

JAYNE
How come they're preserved?

MAL
Place must've gone hermetic when the power blew. Sealed 'em.

KAYLEE
(very upset)
What're they doing? What's everybody doing?

SIMON
There's no discoloration, nobody's doubled over or showing signs of pain...

MAL
There's gasses that kill painless, right?

INARA
But they didn't fall down.
None of them. They just lay down.

SIMON
More than anything, it looks like starvation.

MAL
Anybody want to bet there's plenty of food around?

INARA
They just lay down...

They notice River now, in the middle of the street, keening. She drops to her knees, clutching her

Above and opposite:
Concept art of a deserted
city street is reproduced on
location.

head. As she speaks we see, as
she sees:

INT./EXT. FLASHBACKS

FLASHES: bodies. In homes, in
piles: an entire world, gently
dead.

EXT. CITY - DAY

RIVER
(Chinese)
RUNtse duh SHANG-DEE, ching
DAIwuhtzo,
*[English: Merciful God please take
me away]*
make them stop, they're
everywhere, every city every
house every room, they're all
inside me, I can hear them
all and they're saying nothing!
GET UP! PLEASE, GET
THEM UP! WUOshang mayer,
maysheen, BYEN shr-to,
*[English: I will close my ears
and my heart and I will be
a stone]*
please God make me a stone...

JAYNE
(upset)
She's starting to damage my calm.

ZOE
Jayne —

JAYNE
She's right! Everybody's dead! This
whole world is dead for no reason!

WASH
Let's get to the beacon.

EXT. LANDING STRIP - DAY

It's small — landing is easier in
cities with flying vehicles. At the
end of a short runway, tipped and
damaged, is an Alliance Research
Vessel. The gang makes its way
towards it.

INT. RESEARCH VESSEL - DAY

It's a mess, doors pried open, signs
of violence but no bodies. The
gang walks through it, looking
around.

River pulls away from Simon, suddenly determined. She approaches
a console, and a small disc-like
object. She turns it slightly –

A hologram squawks to life amidst
them all. First we see images that

resemble the flashes from River's
mind: Corpses, everywhere. We
hear and then see DOCTOR
CARON standing exactly where
she was when she recorded this
message...

(As she speaks, we see angles of
everyone watching, taking it in...
River silently mouths every word.)

CARON
— just a few of the images we've
recorded, and you can see it
isn't... it isn't what we thought.
There's been no war here, and no
terraforming event. The environment is stable. It's the Pax, the G-
32 Paxilon Hydroclorate that we
added to the air processors. It's...
(tearing up)
...well it works... it was supposed
to calm the population, weed out
aggression. Make a peaceful... it
worked. The people here stopped
fighting. And then they stopped
everything else. They stopped
going to work, stopped breeding...
talking... eating...
(trying for control)
There's thirty million people here
and they all just let themselves
die. They didn't even kill them-

selves. They just... most starved. When they stopped working the power grids, there were overloads, fires — people burned to death sitting in their chairs. Just sitting.

There is a loud bang somewhere behind her — she starts, gathers herself.

CARON
I have to be quick. There was no one working the receptors when we landed, so we hit pretty hard. We can't leave. We can't take any of the local transports because...

The bang again.

CARON
There are people... they're not people... about a tenth of a percent of the population had the opposite reaction to the Pax. Their aggressor response increased... beyond madness. They've become... they've killed most of us... not just killed, they've done... things.

WASH
(quietly)
Reavers... they made them...

CARON
I won't live to report this, and we haven't got power to... people have to know...
(loses it here)
... We meant it for the best... to make people safer... to... God!

She whirls, grabs a gun and fires — then aims the gun at her own head — but a Reaver is on her, knocks the gun away and bites her face —

She screams continuously as the Reaver tops her, biting at her and tearing at her clothes, at her skin.

JAYNE
(quietly)
Turn it off.

Wash does, nobody saying anything.

Mal walks outside.

EXT. RESEARCH VESSEL - CONTINUING

He takes a few unsteady steps away from the vessel. Inara appears behind him, follows — he holds a hand out behind him, seemingly to make her stop, but then he grabs her shoulder, holds her for support. She puts her hand over his.

MAL
I seen so much death... I been on fields carpeted with bodies, friends and enemies — I seen men and women blown to messes no further from me than you.

INARA
Mal...

MAL
But every single one of those people died on their feet. Fighting. Or, hell, running away — doing summat to get through. This is...

INARA
Mal, I need your help with this. I need you to help me, because I can't —

He looks at her, folds her into his arms. Brings her face to his, not kissing but touching, pressing into each other with the urgency of pulsing, necessary life.

INT. RESEARCH VESSEL - CONTINUING

River falls to her knees, vomiting. Simon goes to her, puts his hand on her back, lets her ride it out.

SIMON
River...

RIVER
I'm all right.

She looks at him, wet eyes full of clarity.

RIVER
I'm all right.

Wash pulls the recording cylinder out of the console.

INT. SERENITY - DINING ROOM - NIGHT

The cylinder is on the table. Mal stands at the head, looking at his crew.

MAL
This report is maybe twelve years old. Parliament buried it, and it stayed buried til River dug it up. This is what they feared she knew. And they were right to fear, 'cause there's a universe of folk that are gonna know it too. (touches the cylinder)
They're gonna see it. Somebody has to speak for these people.

He pauses. Everyone waits.

MAL
You all got on this boat for different reasons, but you all come to the same place. So now I'm asking more of you than I have before. Maybe all. 'Cause as sure as I know anything I know this: They will try again. Maybe on another world, maybe on this very ground, swept clean. A year from now, ten, they'll swing back to the belief that they can make people... better. And I do not hold to that. So no more running. I aim to misbehave.

There is a beat as he eyes them all.

JAYNE
Shepherd Book used to tell me: if you can't do something smart, do something right.

By way of emphasis he takes a big swig of something in a clay jar. Mal takes in the fact that Jayne has spoken for them all. Jayne slides the jar over to Simon, who catches it —

SIMON
Do we have a plan?

MAL
Mr Universe. We haven't the equipment to broadwave this code, but he can put it on every screen for thirty worlds. He's pretty damn close, too.

Simon drinks during this, then looks at the jar suspiciously.

RIVER
Based on our orbital trajectories, he reached optimum proximity just before our sunset. If we make a direct run within the hour we're only 367,442 miles out. At full burn we'd reach him inside of four hours.

She doesn't notice the reactions to her sudden clarity — she's still somewhat in her own world.

WASH
Still got the Reavers, and probably the Alliance between us and him.

ZOE
It's a fair bet the Alliance knows about Mr Universe. They're gonna see this coming.

MAL
No.

He takes a long moment, his jaw tightening imperceptibly.

MAL
They're not gonna see this coming.

EXT. SERENITY ENGINE - VFX - DAY

CLOSE ON: One of Serenity's jet engines, as it FIRES up.

EXT. CITY - DAY

Serenity is taking off, leaving the dead place behind.

INT. MR UNIVERSE'S HQ - CONTINUING

He's talking with Mal and Wash again, very animated.

MR UNIVERSE
It's no problem! Bring it on bring it on bring it on! From here to the eyes and ears of the 'verse, that's my motto, or it might be if I start having a motto.

MAL (ON SCREEN)
We won't be long.

MR UNIVERSE
You're gonna get caught in the ion

cloud, it'll play merry hob with your radar, but pretty pretty lights and a few miles after you'll be right in my orbit.

MAL (ON SCREEN)
You'll let us know if anyone else comes at you?

DROP BACK WIDE to see: The Operative, the Ensign and eight soldiers are in the room, visible to Mr Universe but not to the screen.

MR UNIVERSE
You'll be the first.

A beat, and he turns in his chair to the Operative:

MR UNIVERSE
There. Toss me my thirty coin but I got a newswave for you, friend —

The Operative stabs him through, face clenched with intensity. Mr Universe looks at him, "what the hell'd you do that for?", and The Operative's expression softens, also becoming confused.

He pulls his sword out and looks at it, surprised by this display of emotion, as Mr Universe slumps over.

THE OPERATIVE
(to the Ensign, distracted)
Call in every ship in the quadrant. We'll meet them in the air.

He sets himself — job to do. To the soldiers:

THE OPERATIVE
Destroy it all.

EXT. SPACE - VFX - NIGHT

We are amongst the Reaver armada. Serenity slices quietly through the ships, as we come around and see Miranda receding in the distance.

Serenity drifts through the armada — and suddenly another ship fires up, running next to her...

The two ships pace each other, another vessel coming about as though staring at Serenity, who comes closer and closer to frame, till we see:

EXT. SERENITY/CANNON - NIGHT

The suited corpse draped on the cannon. It suddenly moves: it's Mal.

He swings the cannon round and fires at the ship pacing them. It

IL MADOC REES '04 SERENITY 'V2

Above: Pre-production art of the fully Reavered out Serenity emerging from the ion cloud, with the Reaver armada in pursuit.

BLOWS, fragmenting into burning bits that spiral into other ships, causing two smaller ones to blow as well.

Mal swings around and fires at another ship.

EXT. SATELLITE - VFX - NIGHT

In close orbit waits the Alliance force, at least fifty strong, and clearly with high tech firepower. We move in on the Operative's ship, in the middle of the cluster.

INT. THE OPERATIVE'S SHIP - BRIDGE - CONTINUING

As the Operative waits with the others.

HELMSMAN
I'm reading activity in the cloud.

THE OPERATIVE
(into com)

Lock and fire on my command.
(to himself)
You should have let me see her.
We should have done this as men.
Not with fire...

HELMSMAN
Sir!

EXT. SPACE - VFX - CONTINUING

It's the Operative's POV: the swirling Ion cloud as Serenity breaks through and heads at us, fully Reavered out.

INT. THE OPERATIVE'S SHIP - BRIDGE - CONTINUING

He looks confused, then smiles at the ruse. Hits the com:

THE OPERATIVE
Vessel in range, lock on...
(admiringly)
Bastard's not even changing course...

EXT. SPACE - VFX - CONTINUING

As Serenity gets a bit closer, FIFTY REAVER SHIPS suddenly burst from the cloud, also heading straight at us.

INT. THE OPERATIVE'S SHIP - BRIDGE - CONTINUING

The Operative — and everyone around him - goes big-eyed.

THE OPERATIVE
That's not good...

HELMSMAN
(freaking)
Sir?

THE OPERATIVE
Target the Reavers!
(into com)
Target the Reavers! Target everyone! Somebody FIRE!

EXT. SPACE - VFX - CONTINUING

WASH
(to himself)
I am a leaf on the wind, watch
how I soar.

EXT. SPACE - VFX - CONTINUING

Serenity slips right under the
Operative's ship and ducks and
weaves between dozens more.
The Reaver force hits the Alliance
head on — and several ships do
just that, smashing into bigger
ships kamikaze-style, everything
exploding —

The fleet mobilizes, blasting
Reaver ships, circling around, and
an air war begins, a frenzied, bal-
letic ecstasy of destruction that
the camera hurtles through as
ships and parts of ships fly at and
past it.

ANGLE: SERENITY

She nearly makes it all the way
through the Alliance fleet before
a barrelling chunk of debris —
which is twice their size — forces
them to come hard about and
remain in the fray.

Serenity suddenly lists hard to
port — until she's almost upside
down — the Alliance ships FIRE,
missing Serenity but tagging a
few Reaver ships, none of whom
have slowed down —

**INT. SERENITY BRIDGE -
CONTINUING**

Mal is back on the bridge as we
look out at the upside down
Alliance fleet, missiles just passing us —

MAL
We're too close for them
to arm —

ZOE
This is gonna be very tight —

JAYNE
(entering)
Hey look, we're upside down.

Zoe and Mal shoot a look at Jayne.

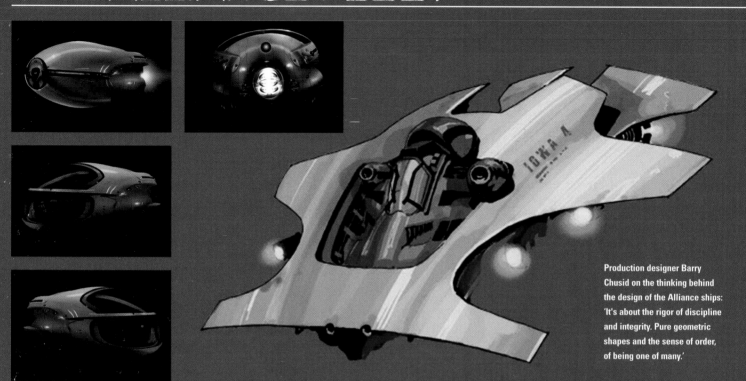

Production designer Barry Chusid on the thinking behind the design of the Alliance ships: 'It's about the rigor of discipline and integrity. Pure geometric shapes and the sense of order, of being one of many.'

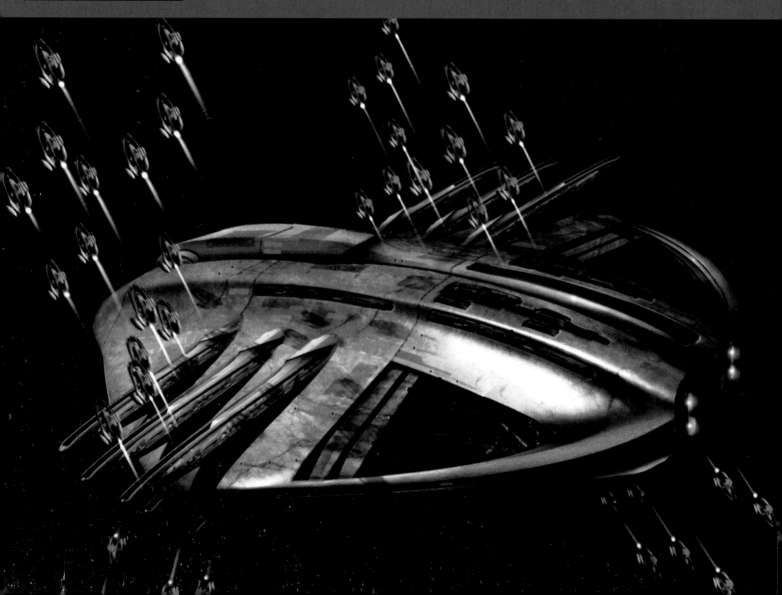

everything you were... how did
you go on?

Mal hits the button to close the
inner doors, steps inside as they
slide together. Glances at the
Operative, unimpressed.

MAL
You still standing there when the
engine starts, you never will figure it
out.

The Operative watches the door
shut. A moment, and he goes.

INT. CARGO BAY - CONTINUING

Mal stows the gear as Zoe
approaches.

MAL
(to himself)
What a whiner...

ZOE
Sir, we have a green light.
Inspection's pos and we're clear
for upthrust.

MAL
Think she'll hold together?

ZOE
She's tore up plenty. But she'll fly
true.

A beat between them before:

MAL
Make sure everything's secure.
Could be bumpy.

ZOE
Always is.

She takes off and Mal heads up
the stairs.

**INT. FOREDECK HALL -
CONTINUING**

Mal comes in and runs into Inara.
Jayne passes through as they talk,
eating a bowl of rice and heading
down into his bunk. Pays them no
mind. Neither do Simon and Kaylee,
in the dining room stowing
supplies.

MAL
We're taking her out. Should be
about a day's ride to get you back to
your girls.

INARA
Right.

MAL
(moving past her)
You ready to get off this heap and
back to a civilized life?

INARA
I, uh...
(he stops)
I don't know.

He looks at her, a smile in his eyes.

MAL
Good answer.

He turns and heads into the bridge.

INT. BRIDGE - CONTINUING

Mal eases himself into his seat.
Takes a moment to adjust one of

**EXT. REPAIR YARD/
SERENITY - DAY**

It's raining as Mal is hauling in the last of the repair equipment. The camera moves around him, skirting the ground of the junkyard, till it lands on a figure in foreground, standing watching him from some twenty feet away.

Mal stops, doesn't turn. Hand near his gun.

MAL
If you're here to tell me we ain't finished... then we will be real quick.

The Operative stands just under the canopy of the nose of the ship, framed by the rain behind.

THE OPERATIVE
Do you know what an uproar you've caused? Protests, riots — cries for a recall of the entire Parliament.

MAL
(turning)
We've seen the broadwaves.

THE OPERATIVE
You must be pleased.

MAL
'Verse wakes up a spell. Won't be long 'fore she rolls right over and falls back asleep. T'aint my worry.

THE OPERATIVE
I can't guarantee they won't come after you. The Parliament. They have a hundred men like me and they are not forgiving.

MAL
That don't bode especially well for you... giving the order to let us go, patching up our hurt...

THE OPERATIVE
I told them the Tams were no longer a threat — damage done.

They might listen, but... I think they know I'm no longer their man.

MAL
They take you down, I don't expect to grieve overmuch. Like to kill you myself, I see you again.

THE OPERATIVE
You won't. There is...
(small, grim smile)
...nothing left to see.

Mal looks at him a moment, then picks up his gear to head inside. The Operative starts away into the rain, then stops to look up at the nose of the ship.

ANGLE: the newly painted Serenity, standing tall in the rain.

THE OPERATIVE
"Serenity". You lost everything in that battle. Everything you had,

Opposite top and above:
'Inara repaints the name on the nose with elegant precision.'

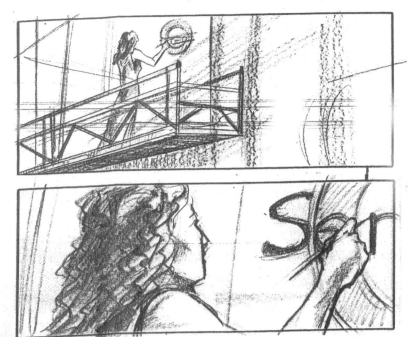

INT. DUCT INSIDE SERENITY - DAY

We are close on River as she works inside a crawlspace just above the engine room, replacing wires. Some of them run to a computer screen that she checks and adjusts.

EXT. REPAIR YARD/TOP OF SERENITY - DAY

Mal and Jayne hold onto the cannon as a crane is lifting it off the top of the ship.

Close on Mal as he watches it go...

WIDER ANGLE:

EXT. REPAIR YARD - CONTINUING

And here we see the whole ship for the first time, harnessed by the wings above the ground so she can be worked on all over. The cannon is being hoisted away from her as a crew of repairmen wheel new landing gear under her belly.

INT. ENGINE ROOM - DAY

Kaylee, deeply greasy, tweaks a part on the engine and crosses to the back where Simon, shirtless and not entirely ungreasy himself, is wrenching a bolt into place above his head. A moment looking at him and she can't help herself — she slides her arms around his chest...

EXT. SERENITY - DAY

On a scaffold, Inara repaints the name on the nose with elegant precision.

INT. ENGINE ROOM - DAY

Kaylee and Simon are just making out like fiends, work completely forgotten. With nothing resembling elegant precision, they sink out of frame to the floor.

A beat, and River's head appears from the crawlspace above, looking down at them with detached curiosity.

INT. BASEMENT, OVER THE GENERATOR - CONTINUING

The Operative sits in silence, the voices coming over his com:

SOLDIER (O.S.)
Targets are acquired! Do we have a kill order? Do we have an order?

INT. BLACK ROOM - CONTINUING

CLOSE ON: THE SOLDIER'S FINGER, SQUEEZING THE TRIGGER...

BLACK OUT.

EXT. DESERT PLANET - SUNSET

We are close on a gravestone. It is rounded, looks more like a bell than a headstone. It is topped by a jar built into the stone. The jar is weathered tin at top and bottom, but glass in the middle. Inside the glass we can see one of those slightly moving photos. It is of Mr Universe and his lovebot, and the name Mr Universe is carved roughly in the stone beneath.

The camera moves to the right and we see another such stone, this one bearing the image and inscription: Shepherd Derrial Book.

The third is Hoban Washburne. Wash.

The camera continues moving right, but the next stone houses a small home-made rocket with pieces of paper taped to it instead of a picture-jar. And fixing another slip of paper to it is River.

She moves away from the stone as Mal does likewise. They're flanked by the crew: Jayne, Inara (to whom Mal moves), Simon, who stands holding River before him and hand in hand with Kaylee. He has a crutch supporting his other side.

There is a moment, then they all move aside, saying nothing. Between them walks Zoe, in a sim-ple white funeral gown, holding a burning taper.

She stands at the stones a moment, then holds the taper to the rocket fuse. Stands back with the others.

The rocket shoots up into the dark-ening sky. They all watch its sputter-ing tail a moment, then it it explodes in a series of fireworks.

WIDE ON the group, as the fire-works go off over their heads.

We are close on another explosion when it becomes:

CLOSE ON: A BLOWTORCH spitting sparks. Widen to see:

EXT. REPAIR YARD/SERENITY - DAY

Zoe is harnessed to the nose of the ship, welding on a replace-ment for the very window the harpoon that impaled Wash came through.

Below: The funeral scene is one of Joss Whedon's favourites in the film: 'It's the most beautiful colors and skin tones and feeling I've ever seen.'